T

God's Gift

—————•◆•—————

Jill Fuller

In gratitude for times spent with
Ida Rix (October 1905 to January 2005)
and
Branwen Hogg (April 1942 to January 2005)

First published in Great Britain in 2006

Society for Promoting Christian Knowledge
36 Causton Street
London SW1P 4ST

British Library Cataloguing-in-Publication Data
A catalogue record for this book is available from the British Library

ISBN-13: 978–0–281–05750–4
ISBN-10: 0–281–05750–8

1 3 5 7 9 10 8 6 4 2

Typeset by Graphicraft Ltd., Hong Kong
Printed in Great Britain by Bookmarque Ltd, Croydon, Surrey

Jill Fuller is currently a freelance writer. She has taught in urban and rural primary and secondary schools, and has also run retreat days and led workshops for teachers and ordinands. As well as having contributed to several publications and written for various organizations, Jill is the author of a number of books concerning children's worship, religious education and spirituality. *John's Book* is a novel she published to help children come to terms with the death of a parent. She is married with two adult children.

Contents

———•◆•———

Acknowledgements

There are many people who have helped in the development and completion of this book and I am extremely grateful for the kindness and encouragement I have received. It was while I was preparing to lead a Quiet Day for a group of headteachers of church schools on the theme of Time that some of the ideas for this book developed. I would like to thank Verity Holloway of Salisbury Diocesan Board of Education for the opportunity this invitation provided. It was a great privilege to share time with a group of people who were themselves under great pressures of time but were committed to both their own faith journey and providing a nurturing environment for the spiritual development of the staff and pupils under their care.

My thanks are also due to Gordon Lamont for his support and help. I am particularly indebted to Alison Barr, Senior Editor of SPCK, for her great patience and her ability to convey gentle reassurance over the telephone. On the practical side, Richard Weldon of Swainscombe Computers was a tower of strength and calmed me down at the times when I thought I had lost everything to the ether.

The stories in the book inevitably derive a great deal from my own spiritual journey and from sharing the journeys of others. Some stories are completely imaginary, some bear the fingerprints of my own experiences and just a few are true. My deepest thanks are to my husband John, my steadfast friend and best critic who has shared all the significant stories and meaningful times of my life and whose companionship and unconditional love sustain me and make the time of my life such fun.

All biblical quotations are from the New English Bible or the Revised Standard Version.

Introduction

We all live within the constraints of time balancing the demands of work, relationships and our own need for space and recreation. Much is written about the management of our time, encouraging us to use time efficiently and to plan our time to ensure 'effective outcomes'. We also live in an era when activity, 'busy-ness' and speed are given a high value. A full diary is seen as success, an instant response as decisiveness, a hurried demeanour reckoned as evidence of a purposeful and important engagement. Increasingly people are being urged towards a 24/7 lifestyle, and even the vocabulary describing the time left for recreation has absorbed an atmosphere of obligation. Holidays are part of the leisure 'industry' and relaxation and sport have become part of an exercise 'regime'.

Whilst efficiency and industry are both valuable and can enhance our achievements, there is a tendency that, in an overactive environment, time can be seen as an enemy and our lives become an anxious race against the clock, straining to beat its demands and fearful lest we 'lose' time or fall behind the targets and goals set us. This book invites us to examine the ways we experience time and to reassess it as a gift from God, a space within which we discover our path of discipleship and live out God's purposes for us. It aims to raise awareness of our attitudes towards time, and explore how these underlying perceptions can affect the way we live our lives and influence the people we become. It encourages us to free ourselves from fear of time, to step beyond views of time which confine our life, and to place our time trustingly within the context of our relationship with God. It asks us to embrace time as God's gift in a busy world and to recognize the time given to us as a unique opportunity to discover our divine humanity.

How the book works

Each Session has two parts. In the first part of each Session the theme is developed and an aspect of time is explored through stories which relate to everyday experiences. In the second part of each Session there are reflective exercises which can be used to aid further consideration of the theme.

Choosing how to use the book

The book could be used:

- as the basis for a group Quiet Day or series of Quiet Days;
- as material for a weekly discussion group over a period of six weeks or an occasional discussion group spread over a longer period;
- for personal devotion or as an aid to an individual retreat.

At the end of the book is a section called 'Guidance for Group Leaders'. There are also suggestions for music which might help the individual or group to focus on the theme and poetry for further exploration of each Session. There is a format for a 'Closing Worship' suitable for a group to use together at the end of the six Sessions.

Making use of the stories and reflective exercises

You may find it helpful to keep a notebook or journal to jot down ideas, questions and insights as you progress through the book.

Each Session has a number of stories in it which are related to the theme. Exploring the story and how it affects you or links with your experience might be as productive as using the exercises. You may like to record your feelings about the stories in your notebook or to write a story from your own lifetime which is related to the theme.

There are several reflective exercises in each Session, so the choice is yours. Some exercises take only a few moments but others need a little time to assemble materials and could continue over a longer period. There are no rules about how to use this section! Often you may choose to spend longer on one exercise, or choose to do none of them. It is your journey and exploration, so only do what feels life-giving to you at that point. You can always return to the exercises at another time.

Gathering the fruits of your time

Always leave yourself a few moments to gather together how the Session has affected your thinking and feeling and how it might influence the way you use your time. The following questions may be useful:

- What have I learnt from this Session? What new insights about the place of time in my life have I gleaned?
- How might these insights affect my attitudes towards time and affect how I live my daily life?
- Are there actions I need to take to follow this through?

There is a concluding prayer at the end of the first part of each Session. Use this to end your time of reflection.

SESSION 1

There is no time

This Session explores:

- our attitudes towards time
- how we choose to use and value time

Part 1

Say the word 'time' to anyone, and what feelings and pictures are immediately aroused? Is it of lazy afternoons relaxing in the summer sun, an evening curled up absorbed in a book, or time spent chatting with friends over a delicious meal? Alternatively, does the word 'time' conjure up images of alarm clocks startling you from sleep, anxious sprints for trains or scanning diaries to find those strangely named 'windows of opportunity'? All these pictures concern time and how we use it, but for many today time is associated with anxiety and a sense of hurried rush rather than the quiet appreciation of the moment.

People have always marked the passage of time, whether by sunrise and sunset, burning measured candles, the angelus bell in monastic life or the 'knocker up' waking the workers for another day in the factory. We have, by one means or another, sought to impose rhythm and order into our days. The coming of Standard Time, however, added another dimension. It meant that we all kept to the same time and that we could be required to account for where we were, when, and what we were doing in a far more exact way. There are, of course, advantages. We can arrange meetings without hanging around for someone on a different time-scale, ensure that planes and trains don't collide, be pretty sure that a TV programme billed for 19.30 will be broadcast then. But precise measuring of time has had disadvantages too. We have sliced our time into ever-diminishing slivers, measuring it as a commodity like cheese and using the same vocabulary we adopt when speaking of money. We speak of spending time, wasting time, losing time, saving time and buying time. Time is sometimes seen as synonymous with money, and indeed the phrase 'time is money' has long since entered into common parlance. The origins of that phrase were apparently in the sixteenth century – a period when the rise of trade and the movement of goods would affect the profits of the merchants. Perishable goods would be ruined if not delivered swiftly; profits would be enlarged if two deliveries could be made instead of one.

With this link of time and money, the race against time begins. Instead of seeing time as a gift, the span of our days from birth to death, we treat it as a commodity, a currency with which we bargain and exchange our life for money or goods. As Wordsworth wrote, 'Getting and spending, we lay waste our powers'. We no longer hold our days in the palms of our hands, regarding them as precious jewels, but rather fear that some tyrant, possibly envisioned as an old man with a scythe, will cut us down, forcing us to let time slip through our fingers like sand. Instead of feeling that we have all the time in the world, we fear that we have no time at all and so we rush to contain it, control it, manage it and 'fit more in'. We become seduced by 'time-saving' gadgets, 'fast' food, 'short' cuts through traffic, as if in doing things faster we protect the present moment from the ravages of 'time'. In reality we have 'more time' available than our fellow humans who spend hours of every day walking to and fro to collect water, whilst we have water 'on tap'. We have innumerable household appliances which release us from the everyday tasks of washing and cleaning which took hours of every day for our great-grandparents. But somehow this release from chores does not relieve our anxiety that time is too short, that we are behind and chasing minutes, perpetually rushing and trying to catch up, like the White Rabbit looking at his watch and exclaiming, 'I'm late. I'm late!'

It was nine o'clock. Sally took her coffee into the sitting-room and slumped exhausted in the chair. Where had the day gone? Was it really fourteen hours since she had left the house? The day had seemed a continual whirl of activity. She couldn't remember eating breakfast, though the dirty bowl and cup on the draining board was evidence that she had. The journey to work through the countryside had passed unnoticed. Were the beech trees in leaf yet or were the bluebells out in the woods? She had not noticed. And what of the day? She had scolded her secretary for not having the documents ready. But what was that she had murmured? Something about her sister in hospital? Sally hadn't attended. She had chaired the meeting and her proposals had been accepted, but had she really communicated with her colleagues, listened to their comments, valued their criticisms? The day had gone. She had chased it from dawn to sunset, filling every moment, but somehow she felt like a frenetic and unskilled butterfly catcher; the net she had so wildly flailed around was heavy with emptiness.

It is perhaps only when we are at rock bottom, overwhelmed by busyness, exhausted by continual activity, burdened by the tasks which fill our lives, that we, if not fearing for our lives, at least fearing for the *meaning* of our lives, like Elijah, run away and metaphorically hide in a cave. Then, when we allow ourselves space to pause and reflect, to be still and listen, perhaps we too can hear the still small voice. But this quiet voice is there all the time, inviting us to rest and 'know' even amidst the surrounding rush and turmoil. It is when we allow ourselves to step out of time and to be still that we give ourselves the opportunity to sense again the ever-present reality of God. We can in silence hear the invitation to lay down our burdens and rest in the assurance that God, the Creator of sunrise and sunset, day and night, the hours and the seasons, is also *our* Creator and that the time of our lives is held and sustained by that creative love. It is also that grace and energy, not our efforts and straining, which sustains the world and 'all that therein is'. For those of us whose personality type tips us towards activity and responsibility, this may come as a shock! We need to recognize that it is not a dereliction of duty to stop and pause and to humbly admit that we are human, fallible and limited. Only when we fully acknowledge this and allow God to be God will we reach balance in our lives and fill our time wisely and well. The Psalmist reminds us:

> Unless the Lord builds the house,
> its builders will have toiled in vain.
> Unless the Lord keeps watch over a city,
> in vain the watchman stands on guard.
> In vain you rise up early and go late to rest,
> toiling for the bread you eat;
> he supplies the needs of those he loves.
>
> (Psalm 127.1–2 NEB)

The Christian life is not about proving ourselves by activity but rather seeking to discern what that activity should be. This demands that we reserve time to attend to the voice of God within. It involves listening carefully and following the prompts which nudge us towards our true vocation. We are asked not just to fill our days with good works, worthy as they might be, but to continually seek out God's purposes for us and use the abundant time we are given in life-giving ways.

The story of Martha and Mary in Luke 10.38–42 is sometimes interpreted as portraying a tension between activity and contemplation and as a rebuke for spending time on the mundane necessities of life instead of sitting at the feet of Christ. Those of us who have spent a great deal of time preparing food and washing up may be forgiven for having a great deal of sympathy with Martha. Understandably we feel solidarity with 'Martha the Worker', castigating Mary with scornful 'It's all right for her!' comments.

But when we look at the story more closely, we recognize Christ's challenge more clearly. He was always asking his followers to look afresh at their priorities, seeking to release them from stereotyped role models and inherited expectations. Was he challenging Martha not to abandon the real and necessary chores of the day, but rather to discern more accurately the true priorities, to discover her 'better part'? Was he daring her to find her real self, her own gifts, the true way she was meant to spend her time? Was Martha so hard done by, or does she represent that part of our own personality which imprisons ourselves by refusing to risk stepping out of inherited patterns and role models, and instead chooses to conform to the expectations of the age?

Here in the twenty-first century, part of this expectation may be a preoccupation with activity and with measurable results. So often we choose to use our time by succumbing to the immediate demand rather than the longer vision. We respond to the urgent task, the present issue rather than seek out what is our eternal vocation. The pressures to concur with accepted values are strong. We need to be continually alert to how current values influence our decisions about how we spend our time. Are we finding our security by using our time and energies to seek the approval of others, or perhaps to obtain power, financial success or celebrity? God is always calling us to leave behind those attitudes and presuppositions which could enslave us. He wants us to travel on in faith and in the freedom of his love, to make life-giving choices about how we spend the time we are given. 'I came that they may have life, and have it abundantly' (John 10.10 RSV).

Tony watched the group of children as they crowded into the carriage of the tube. They were excited, chattering to each other, alert to everything around them. He surmised that they were on a school visit, perhaps to a museum or art gallery. The young boy nearest him had a tell-tale clip-board sticking out of his bulging haversack. The teacher was talking to them, sharing jokes, his eyes continually checking his young charges. They got off at the next stop and the carriage seemed strangely quiet, dull and lifeless.

Tony resumed his mid-space stare, avoiding eye contact with other passengers, the expected behaviour of regular commuters on the underground. As the train jolted onwards he found himself reflecting on his own school days, the friends he had had, his interests, how he had spent his days. He remembered how his life had seemed to stretch ahead of him, waiting for choices to be made, opportunities taken, adventures embarked upon. Life had seemed full of amazing possibilities then. So how had he ended up in a grey suit working for a firm whose ethos he disliked and whose values he despised?

He looked back at the choices he had made along the way and, more importantly, the attitudes which had driven those choices. He recognized that he had always felt obliged to 'succeed' without really considering how he measured success. He had felt a need to make money without ever questioning what he wanted the money for. He had felt a pressure to gain the approval of others, to make 'safe' choices which led to a house in a leafy suburb, a good income, a respected place in the community, a certain status. And so that was how he had spent his time – choosing friends who could help him acquire power and influence, chasing contracts which brought him kudos regardless of the real cost, seeking promotions which appeared to represent more power. What was his life's work adding up to? The tube sighed into the next station. Tony got up. It was the place to change trains.

In reflecting on time, we need to regularly remind ourselves that we live in God's world and God's time. This span of time has been given us to rejoice and marvel at God's creation and to become the person God wants us to be. Our worth lies in that we have been created by a loving God, are loved by God and will return to the source of that love. God gives us time and it is in God's time that we live our lives. Psalm 23 is often said or sung at funerals, the end of a person's allotted time on earth. Yet the psalm gives a vision of what it is like to live now, in the present moment, with an understanding of a loving God who invites us to dwell with him 'all the days' of our lives. Here is a poetic vision of a God as a shepherd who is not harrying us along and goading us to eat faster or walk more quickly, but one who encourages us to 'lie down in green pastures'. This is not a shepherd who terrifies us with tales of wicked wolves or alarms us with fears of precipitous falls over unseen cliffs. This is the 'Good Shepherd' who is himself our provider, guide and protector. He provides waters of peace for us to rest by. He renews our energy and reassures us when we are beset with problems. He comforts us and encourages us to overcome our fears. When we allow ourselves to refresh ourselves by these still waters, then we may have a new vision of time and eternity and see that there is all the time in the world.

> An old woman approached the gates of Heaven. As she drew nearer she pondered on what kind of reception she would receive. Would God commend her for the floors she had scrubbed, the people she had helped, the worthy causes on whose committees she had served? Or would he condemn her for not weeding the garden, ignoring the telephone and refusing to be on the PCC?
>
> As the gates swung open she saw God running towards her with open arms, calling out, 'Ah, my dear, welcome! Tell me, did you enjoy the time I gave you in my world?'

Concluding prayer

Gracious God, the Alpha and Omega, the Beginning and the End
We thank you for this present moment
For this unrepeatable hour of the day
For this unique day of the week

There is no time

For this month of the year's seasons
For this special year in eternity.
Help us to rejoice in the gift of time you have given us
Neither fretting about time past
Nor straining to achieve future goals
But rather coming into your presence
Resting in your time.

Gracious God, whose breath enlivens us, granting us our
    daily life
Enlighten our choices as to how we spend our time
Give us insight into our motivations
Discernment in choosing our paths
Courage in taking hard decisions.
Anoint us with the oil of your peace
Enable us with love
Strengthen us with faith
So may we dwell in your presence all the days of our lives.
Amen.

Part 2
Reflections and exercises on Session 1,
'There is no time'

1 Letting God be God

The words for 'spirit' in Greek (*pneuma*), Hebrew (*ruach*) and Latin (*spiritus*) are all linked to the word for 'breath'. We tend to take our breath for granted, only noticing it when we are short of breath, out of breath, breath-less. Yet this un-noticed part of our daily living is essential to our well-being and continuance. Anyone who has witnessed the first cry of a newborn baby or waited by the bed of the dying will know the sheer miracle of breath which separates life from death. From the second of our birth to our last moments, our breathing mechanism allows us to take in fresh oxygen and expel waste carbon dioxide. It is indeed the living spirit of our life.

Just as we ignore this everyday miracle, so too we may fall into the trap of ignoring the presence of God and the still small voice. We need to stop and 'take a deep breath', to utter the prayer, 'Breathe on us, breath of God' and to put our time once more into the awareness of God's presence, to allow God to be God.

Take a few minutes to be aware of your breathing and to sense its rhythm.

Be aware that with each breath in, you take in new life and oxygen.

Allow yourself with each breath out to let go of those tensions around your use of time which prevent you from being fully in the present.

- With each breath in, say to yourself the phrase: 'Breathe on me, breath of God.'
- Then with each breath out: 'Fill me with life anew.'

- Then with each breath in: 'That I may love what Thou dost love.'
- Then with each breath out: 'And do what Thou wouldst do.'

Allow yourself time to imagine God's breath and your breath being one, God's life and Spirit within you refreshing you, sustaining you every moment from the time of your birth to the time of your death.

When you are accustomed to the pattern, you may choose to take several breaths and repeat each phrase three or four times.

You may choose to use other phrases from the selection below or to compose a phrase of your own.

- I am with you always to the end of time (Matthew 28.20 NEB).
- Be still, and know that I am God (Psalm 46.10 RSV).
- Wait for the LORD, be strong, and let your heart take courage (Psalm 27.14 RSV).

You may find it helpful to repeat this exercise daily before praying. Alternatively, it could be used to remind us that we live in God's time when waiting for trains or appointments or at supermarket tills.

2 Martha and Mary

This exercise uses the Ignatian method of entering imaginatively into the biblical text. It could be that the exercise could be spread over a period of time, reading the passage through one night before bed and again on successive days, so that the story and its events are clearly in your mind's eye.

Read the passage in Luke 10.38–42 (NEB). Allow yourself time to imagine the scene. Choose to be either Mary or

Martha. Imagine the preparations for the arrival of Jesus, the plans and expectations. Imagine Jesus arriving and what happened. Allow the events to unfold before you. Watch how you and others are behaving. Notice the body language and eye contact. How do you react to Martha's words, to the words of Jesus? What are Mary's expressions and responses? Bring yourself gently back into the present after this exercise. You may like to consider these questions:

(a) In your daily life at home or at work, how are you 'distracted by many tasks'? How does this prevent you from listening to your inner self and developing your special skills?

Do you ever feel that, like Martha, you are the person who is left 'to get on with the work by' yourself?

If so, what does this reveal about your attitudes to others and to yourself?

How can you respond to this challenge?

Could it mean . . .

- letting go of the reins?
- delegating tasks you feel possessive of?
- having courage to leave some tasks for another time?
- freeing yourself from an image that you, your past or someone else is imposing on you?

(b) Are there things you are 'fretting and fussing' about?

What do you suppose is the 'one thing necessary'?

What is the 'one thing' you feel called to at this point of time?

How can you follow this calling by the way you use time?

(c) 'Mary . . . seated herself at the Lord's feet and stayed there.'

How difficult or easy was it to decide to stay listening to
Jesus?

What was it that drew you to him?

How did you feel about Martha doing the work? Martha's
criticism? Jesus' reassurance?

What have you learnt about your own attitudes to choosing stillness, criticism, approval?

3 Leaving your nets or changing trains?

God continually challenges us to listen to the still, small
voice and calls us to new ways of living, just as he called
those of times past. However, familiarity with the stories
of the Bible can sometimes blind us to the uncomfortable
reality of the courage and faith demanded of those who
responded. We tend to overlook the way that listening to
the inner call of God disrupted the lives of followers. Listen
attentively to the Iona hymn, 'God it was' (available on *Love
From Below*,[1] Iona Worship Group, Iona Community) or
read it below:

> God it was who said to Abraham,
> 'Pack your bags and travel on!'
> God it was who said to Sarah,
> 'Smile and soon you'll bear a son!'
> Travelling folk and aged mothers
> wandering when they thought they'd done –
> this is how we find God's people,
> leaving all because of One.
>
> God it was who said to Moses,
> 'Save my people, part the sea!'
> God it was who said to Miriam,
> 'Sing and dance to show you're free!'

Shepherd-saints and tambourinists
doing what he knew they could –
this is how we find God's people,
liberating what they should.

God it was who said to Joseph,
'Down your tools and take your wife!'
God it was who said to Mary,
'In your womb, I'll start my life!'
Carpenter and country maiden
leaving town and trade and skills –
this is how we find God's people,
Moved by what their Maker wills.

Christ it was who said 'Zacchaeus,
I would like to eat with you!'
Christ it was who said to Martha,
'Listening's what you need to do!'
Civil servants and housekeepers
changing places at a cost –
this is how Christ summons people,
calling both the loved and lost.

In this crowd which spans the ages,
with these saints whom we revere,
God wants us to share their purpose
starting now and starting here.
So we celebrate our calling,
so we raise both heart and voice
as we pray that through our living
more may find they are God's choice.[2]

How is God asking his followers to change what they do with
their time?

What might have been the costs for Abraham, Sarah, Matthew and Martha?

How do you think the cost of following God's call was different for each follower?

How are you being challenged about the way you spend time?

What might be the cost to you of changing those ways?

Are there assumptions about the way you use your time which need revising?

What difficulties might changing your lifestyle present?

Are you feeling 'lost' in the ways you are using your time at this point in your life?

What might Christ challenge you to do in order to redeem the time you have?

4 All the time in the world

At the end of his prayer 'Lord, I have time',[3] Michel Quoist imagines a jug which is being filled to the top with the minutes, hours, days and years of the time God has given us. He imagines the jug being taken to Christ and, as at Cana, Christ transforming the 'water' into an unimagined richness.

Imagine yourself carrying a jug full of water to Christ. Imagine it being transformed into wine. Now think of your time. Think of committing each day into God's hands. What transformations might happen? How might you use all the time God has given you?

SESSION 2

What time is it?

In this Session we look at:

- our attitudes towards past and future time
- the way in which we give value to the distinct stages of our time on earth – childhood, youth, middle age, old age

Part 1

When I was a child my friends and I played a game called 'What's the time, Mr Wolf?' One of us acted the part of the wolf and stood ahead of all the others and with our back towards them. The rest of the group, the chickens, stood behind. The purpose of the game was for the chickens to creep up and touch the wolf without being seen first. This was simple enough but a certain terror was added to the game. The 'chickens' had to repeatedly ask the wolf, 'What's the time, Mr Wolf?' – thus revealing their position. Mr Wolf would obligingly reply, 'Four o'clock', 'Two o'clock' or whatever time came to mind until he shouted 'Supper time!' and turned round to chase and catch the least alert chicken for the imagined feast. If you wanted to remain as a chicken in the game, it was important to be on your toes and aware of the slightest indication that the wolf was about to pounce.

Whilst we are unlikely to be eaten for supper, there is a sense in which we allow ourselves to be 'eaten up' by anxieties about time. We lose the present moment amidst hankerings and regrets about the past, unable to let go of the days we have already lived. Our past can throw long shadows which prevent us standing in the sunshine of today. Alternatively, we can look back at our past with rose-tinted glasses as 'the good old days', preventing ourselves from recognizing and seizing the new opportunities of the moment.

We may also spend quite a lot of the present worrying about the future, about possibilities, fears and hopes. Newspapers and media are full of articles and programmes debating 'what might happen if' someone resigns or a rumour is proved true. Our economic future is to some degree dominated by a stock exchange which is based on balancing probability and possibility and second-guessing the future.

In some ways, inhabiting this space between past and future is our human condition. We are, in our present mortal frame, the link in the time-chain between past and future. The way we use our present moment will have been influenced by our past and is affected by our hopes and fears for the future. Yet to live the present moment well, we need to place a sense of appropriate worth on both past and future, valuing them for what they were or might be, but also being ready to let go of what has been and to face what might be with faith and courage.

As she turned to leave the house for the final time, she heard the ever-present voice which rose unbidden yet again – 'If only . . .' She leaned against the wall of the hall and allowed her mind to rest for a moment on all that the house had meant to her. She could remember the excitement of their early years of marriage and establishing their first home together, the discussions about paint colours and the traumas of attempting to be decorators. This was the place where their children had been born, where they had survived being parents during their offspring's teenage years and from where they had waved them off to college. It had all been so good. And then the second voice whispered – the one she had allowed to tempt her over the past months. What if he changed his mind? What if it didn't work out for him? What if, even as she stood there, he put his key in the lock and asked to come back? Even now, despite the reality of the court, the letters of divorce, the 'For sale' board standing sentinel in the front garden, she found it hard to beat down a foolish hope. She wiped her eyes, checked her handbag yet again and turned to the door. As she closed it she involuntarily recalled a phrase, a saying – was it a prayer? She searched for the partially remembered words: 'For all that has been – Thanks. For all that is to come – Yes!'[4] Who was it who wrote it? She did not know but was grateful for the courage and reality it brought.

When we can recognize and value our past for what it was, warts and all, then we can be released to live today. When we have a realistic vision for our future, then we can utilize the present moment more effectively so that it becomes the gateway to that future. This involves recognizing the reality of being an incarnate body living within a mortal frame, with all the restrictions that imposes. Unlike Dr Who, we cannot enter a time machine. We have a past which we cannot change except by our attitudes to it, and a future which, however we choose to use it, will at some point end. When we can truly accept that 'yesterday is history and tomorrow mystery' we can begin to live today. Many of us struggle with that task daily. Too easily the present moment is filled with tapes which replay scenes of the past which haunt us with fear or regret or perhaps nostalgia. Too often the opportunities of the future are lost through anxieties about our adequacy or strength to meet the challenges and demands which lie ahead.

The Christian hope is that we do not have to face the journey through time alone. Again and again the biblical story tells us of people whose past contained many mistakes and failures, and characters who were not at all respectable or spotless. It also recounts stories of those who felt themselves totally inadequate for the task God was suggesting. 'I am not eloquent . . . I am slow of speech', Moses pleads when terrified by the prospect ahead (Exodus 4.10–13 RSV). But these flawed and anxious people were the very ones God chose to use to further the Kingdom. The mistakes of our past do not make us useless, nor do they either confine or define our future. Christ takes up prostitutes, cheats and swindlers. Feelings of inadequacy or even lack of years and experience are not reasons for turning away from the future God has in mind for us. God entrusts the future of the Church into the hands of one who denied him, and on the Damascus road calls a murderer of Christians to the task of proclaiming his resurrected life. There is nothing in our past which God cannot redeem and use, no past mistake beyond God's love. Nor is there any task ahead to which God calls us which is impossible.

Lying back in the garden chair, Mark had dropped into a fretful sleep. He had felt paralysed by memories and regrets about his past and unable to break free into any future worth the name of life. But now as he awoke there was a strange sense of peace. He lay in that strange space between sleeping and waking and allowed the pictures and experiences of his dreams to return to his mind. He had been, as it were, above himself and looking down on himself, observing his tossing and turning and his restless anxiety.

Then a person who resembled an angel appeared by his side. He followed the angel past a series of doors each one of which was marked with a year of his past life. He drew back, not wanting to look into the rooms behind the doors. He knew how he had struggled with some of the memories of unresolved relationships, unfulfilled hopes, unfinished tasks; the guilt of things he regretted doing and the misery of opportunities missed. He was convinced that behind these past doors lurked dragons he could not face. But as the door swung open, Christ was standing there, and the radiance from his being spread throughout the room. There were no fearful shadows, no dreadful scenes to witness, nothing but a sense of peace and harmony, laughter and acceptance. It was the same with every room they visited. Each season of his life seemed cleansed and healed by the risen Christ.

As they closed the door on the last room, the angel turned and started to move forward. Here the scene was no longer contained within a house. Mark felt the cool wind of the open air and saw a path which was only just visible in a landscape which he could not discern. He hesitated, wanting to turn back and dwell longer in the rooms which now seemed to hold comfort, not terror, but the angel beckoned him on. Surely now that he had dared to face the past, he would be better marking time. His feet felt unsteady and the ground seemed uneven and even treacherous.

But the angel took him by the elbow and pointed ahead. There in the far distance was a clear light. It was not the blazing light of the rooms he had passed through but was sufficient to show the way and to re-assure him that Christ was in the space and time ahead as surely as he had been in the past.

As Mark swung himself upright into the chair and looked around the garden, he reflected on his dream and saw the past and the future in a different light. He did not have to confront his demons alone but with a Christ who had already retraced and redeemed his past and travelled ahead of him, enlightening his future. What was required of him was to recognize that pres-ence and live today in that hope.

Just as the Christian hope redeems our past and encour-ages us to step forward in confidence, so the message of Emmanuel, God with us, means that God's empowering Spirit is not confined to a particular age of our life. God is with us at whatever point in time we are. We are never either too young or too old for God's plans. This is the God who uses Abraham and Sarah, Anna and Simeon, people whose longevity both the writers of Genesis and St Luke were at pains to emphasize. 'Both Abraham and Sarah had grown very old and Sarah was past the age of child-bearing' (Genesis 18.11 NEB). Simeon holds the infant Christ at the temple and thanks the God who 'givest thy servant his dis-charge in peace', whilst Luke goes on to tell us that Anna was 'a very old woman who had lived . . . alone as a widow to the age of eighty-four' (Luke 2.25–38 NEB). Amidst all the crowds of influential, powerful and knowledgeable people who must have frequented the courts of the Temple that day, it is an elderly woman and a frail man approaching death who witness to the presence of the Christ in their midst. There is no ageism in God's personnel management.

> My aunt's hands are no longer beautiful. They are not the plump hands of the child in the sepia photographs over which we pore together. Nor are they the graceful hands of the glamorous war bride in a borrowed wedding dress, clasping the streaming bouquet. They are blue-black in colour, wrinkled and gnarled. They have little strength and are cruelly curved by illness into painful shapes. I watch her carefully balancing her cup or cutting her food with a concentration which betrays the effort she tries to keep hidden beneath a cheerful conversation. These are the hands which volunteered to cook meals nightly for airmen stationed in the village where she lived; the hands which smoothed the sheets of the dying and, early in the morning, helped her father to 'dig for victory'. They are hands which held me securely, steadying me when I might stumble and giving that loving touch which conveyed more than words or looks. Now they rest in her lap, still, inactive, yet to me full of beauty and the quiet wisdom of her experiences. Even in their weakness they speak of courage and love and a faith which endures beyond life's scars.

Just as God recognizes and values old age, so God does not ignore the very young or exclude them from his work. Children have often, like women, been written out of the story and their contributions overlooked. But even a casual glance through the narrative of the Bible shows children taking significant roles. They are bearers of God's messages and are given important parts to play, taking both responsibility and initiative. It is the young girl Miriam who protects Moses; the child Samuel who delivers God's challenging message to Eli; David, described by Saul as 'just a boy', who defeats Goliath; 'a little Israelite girl' who leads Naaman, the powerful commander of the Syrian army, to Elisha; a 'young boy' who offers Christ the loaves and fishes. It is the children who in Matthew 21.14–16 show true insight about Jesus, in contrast to the priests and scribes, who not only fail to recognize him but also object to the children's acclamation. God uses the small and the insignificant and so can use us, however young and apparently powerless we are. How often children open our eyes to the wonder and opportunities amidst the very humdrum experiences of everyday life. Their straight talk can also challenge us with the heart of the gospel message.

After a wonderful Christmas lunch the whole family set out for an afternoon walk. Snow had fallen, and despite the sun, it was crisp and cold. On the way home through the park we passed a sheltered seat. Lying on the bench, covered in newspapers, was a tramp.

'Why is he lying there?' my small son enquired.

'He's sleeping,' I replied.

'Why doesn't he sleep in his bed?'

'He probably hasn't got a bed.'

'Then why don't we ask him home?'

The simplicity of the questioning left me at a loss for a reply. I began several attempts at justifying myself for leaving the tramp in the cold: we had had weeks of visitors before Christmas, parties for Sunday School children, students for meals, and I had been busy baking for this and that charity and good cause.

At the end of my pious catalogue my son replied, 'But that doesn't count. They were your friends.'

I felt as though the voice had spanned the centuries and that I was being reproached by Christ himself: 'If you love only those who love you, what reward can you expect? Surely the tax gatherers do as much as that? And if you greet only your brother, what is there extraordinary about that? Even the heathen do as much. There must be no bounds to your goodness as your heavenly Father's goodness knows no bounds' (Matthew 5.46–47 NEB).

Like the rich young man, I was unable to meet the absolute demands Christ makes of us, but it was my own young child who helped me to see how far I fall short of Christ's discipleship and how easily our 'good works' can disguise what we leave undone.

God can use all our ages, including that 'middle' time when we are both fulfilling our potential but also perhaps feeling stretched between a myriad of conflicting demands.

Carol swung the car into the cul-de-sac and jumped out swiftly. The lights were not yet on in the house so she had just made it before Sophie got home. She was feeling exhilarated. The meeting had gone well, she had felt accepted by her new colleagues and excited by the prospect of fresh challenges. There was a spring in her step as she turned the key in the lock. If only Peter wasn't away again at this busy time.

She put on the kettle and went to listen to the answerphone. It was her maiden aunt: 'I'm sure it's not serious and I don't want you to worry you, but I'm in hospital.'

Carol just had time to make a note of the telephone number when Sophie arrived. 'You haven't forgotten the Concert, have you, Mum?'

'No, I know it's a quick turn-around. There's a snack supper prepared in the fridge for us two, Sam is eating with a friend.'

'Not for me, thanks – we're meeting up early at school. Will is picking me up.'

'Will? Ah yes, he's just passed his test, hasn't he?' Carol fought down the inclination to give Sophie the third degree about driving safely and 'taking care' as she rummaged in the wardrobe and pulled out a dress.

'Mum, you can't wear that, it's just so . . . so, well . . . you just can't.'

'I thought it was the job of parents to be embarrassing to their offspring,' Carol chided.

'Not that embarrassing!' Sophie pleaded. 'Please, Mum, just wear something . . . well . . . ordinary, something which fades into the background. Your navy suit perhaps?'

Carol hung the scarlet dress back and pulled out her safe 'interview' suit. Sophie heaved a sigh of relief. 'Thanks, Mum. Love you,' she said as she clattered down the stairs. 'See you later – don't be late.'

Carol strode into the bathroom, grabbing her mobile on the way; still no message from Sam. She frowned anxiously as she tapped in Sue's number. 'Sue, it's Carol. Has Sam arrived? It's just that he promised to text me. Oh, that's fine. They get involved together – I expect he forgot. So long as he's safe. I'll collect him on the way home – shouldn't be late. And Saturday – it's my turn to take the boys to swimming. Thanks for your help. Bye.'

Later, as she sat in the school hall listening to Sophie play in the orchestra, Carol mused over her day. For once it had worked out OK, but she felt the tiredness of holding it all together creep over her. At this point in time life was a balancing act; exciting and rewarding without doubt, but demanding and complicated too, full of ambiguous situations when choices are complex, situations constantly changing and the way does not always seem clear cut.

The creator God, the source of all our energy and gifts, desires us to reach our potential, to use our time to fully become the person we are in all aspects of our being, physical, emotional, spiritual and intellectual. We are called to love him with all our hearts, minds, strength and soul. The way we use our time at different stages of our life is a response to his invitation to continue the mystery of the dance of life.

God can use us when it seems we are 'in the middle', stretched between caring for the young and the old, holding complex responsibilities and coming to terms with change and compromise. It is perhaps at this point of our lives when our youthful idealism might be fading, when we have to recognize the limitations of our energy levels, when we need to remind ourselves of a God who encompasses the whole spectrum of our lives.

This is a God who not only calls us but travels with us as companion and friend. This is a God who knows about exhaustion and weariness as well as endurance and persistence. He knows the exhilaration of being welcomed as a hero as well as being spat at and perceived as a failure. He understands the Gethsemane of our doubts and fears, the terror that our time may have been meaningless, our choices misguided, our intentions misconstrued, our very being a terrible mistake. He understands the complexities of following a vocation, meeting both approval and derision, the dark side of betrayal, loss of hope and abandonment. With arms outstretched to embrace all our times, he identifies with us, encouraging us to say a vibrant 'Yes' to life at all its stages, redeeming its losses and rejoicing in its gifts.

God has a purpose for us, whatever the time of our life – young, middle aged or elderly. In our youth and inexperience, in our aged frailty and weakness, in the complexities of our middle years God's strength is made incarnate. The God who is the God of all our ages, the Alpha and the Omega, the beginning and the end, who moves with us from past through present to future, can use all the stages of our times creatively if only we will surrender them to his love. Moreover, we have been given the promise that this God is the Good Shepherd who will care for his flock, and this means protecting them from the wolf, even the ravaging wolf of time.

Concluding prayer

Gracious God
Who knew us before we were formed in the womb
Who travels with us through each twist and turn of our lives
Who walks ahead as our guiding light
May we so experience your peace
That we can release our past days into your providence
May we so trust your love
That we can face the future without fear
And so, surrounded by your presence, live today with faith and courage.

Creator God
Who showers us with gifts
May we rejoice at the potential you have given us
Recognizing the varied possibilities of each stage of our life

Gracefully accepting the limitations we have.
So may each age be a witness
To the power of your creative energy.
Amen.

Part 2
Reflections and exercises on Session 2, 'What time is it?

1 Time line

Using a large piece of paper, draw the time line of your life. Mark significant events along the way such as relationships, marriages, births, celebrations, bereavements, moves, health and work. You may like to draw or stick on pictures or use symbols.

Reflect on your time line and consider whether there are still places where the voice 'If only . . .' still haunts you. What do you need to learn from this voice? Observe the pattern of your life *after* the 'If only . . .' experience. In what ways was your life different? Can you recognize any *benefits* to yourself or others from the way your life developed?

With the phrase, 'Consider now the deeds [the Lord] has done for you and give him thanks' (Tobit 13.6) in your mind, use the time line to give thanks for times in your past life. Notice where there are causes for thankfulness even when circumstances were not as you would have planned or hoped for. Can you recognize God's grace in places you previously regarded as desert experiences?

2 Healed rooms

Mark did not want to look into the rooms of his past life, yet when he did so, 'there was nothing but a sense of peace and harmony, laughter and resolution. Each season of his life seemed cleansed and healed by the risen Christ.'

Reflect on whether there are still 'rooms' of your life which you do not want to visit. Imagine Christ standing at the door of that room and giving you the courage and peace to redeem the past events which it contains. It may help to use the following words: 'Thus says the Lord . . . Cease to dwell on days gone by and to brood over past history. Here and now I will do a new thing; this moment it will break from the bud' (Isaiah 43.16, 18–19 NEB).

If some recollections are too painful to face alone, you may choose to do this exercise with a trusted friend or consider how you might choose to use the present time to find help and advice to heal these wounds.

3 New seeds

'Too easily the present moment is filled with tapes which replay scenes of the past which haunt us with fear or regret.' Are there events in your past which you find hard to relinquish? Are there events or hopes or fears which you need to let go of in order to live effectively in the present?

The new life of any plant can only happen when we allow the flowering to finish and the plant to 'go to seed'. What flowers must you now allow to die and how will you nurture the fresh seed? What fresh soil will you need to provide? How will you remember to water the young plant?

You may like to plant some seeds or buy an indoor plant to cherish to symbolize this new beginning.

4 Dreams and visions

'Your old men shall dream dreams and your young men shall see visions' (Joel 2.28 RSV). Think of someone you know who is either very old or quite young. Can you take time to listen to their dreams of the past or their visions for their future? How can you give their dreams and visions value? What have you learned from them?

Perhaps you would like to write down for yourself an appreciation of how they helped you or how their life contributes to the life of the community or the local church. Is there a way you could thank them or show them that you recognize their worth? A letter, a card, or even a short article in the local magazine?

Perhaps you are very old or quite young yourself. Whatever your age, take time to write or draw a dream or vision of your own and share it with someone.

5 What time is it for you?

You may choose to do this exercise with a good friend. Take time to find photographs of yourself at different ages. Reflect on the changes time has brought.

How do you perceive the stage of life you are experiencing now?

How do you see the advantages or disadvantages of this stage of your life?

What particular opportunities are there in being the age you are now?

How might you use the opportunities of this present time creatively?

You might like to make a collage of the photographs of your life entitled 'As time goes by'. Alternatively, you could make a collage of photos and other media which depict your life in the present and entitle it 'This is the day'.

SESSION 3

Sensing time's rhythms

———◆◆◆———

In this Session we consider:

- the natural rhythms of the seasons and day and night
- the rhythm of rest and activity
- the importance of dreaming and reflecting

Part 1

Our lives are surrounded by natural rhythms, day and night, waking and sleeping, the turn of the seasons, birth and death. Newborn babies can be soothed by listening to a tape of sounds from within the womb, the beat of the heart, the pulse of blood moving around the body. Amazingly, babies whose mothers listen to music during pregnancy often show excitement when they hear that same music after birth. It seems that even from before birth we have the capacity to recognize and appreciate rhythm and that rhythm affects us. This sense of rhythm seems to transfer into our evident need of a regular pattern of activity and rest. Whilst the particular pattern may be unique for each individual, the need for the balance between rest and activity, sleep and wakefulness is known by those who use sleep deprivation as a weapon to break resistance to interrogation. It is apparent that we also need the pattern between light and dark, day and night. Our bodies are so finely attuned to the presence or lack of light and sun that some people suffer from SAD (seasonal affect-ive disorder) when deprived of sufficient sunlight. Natural rhythms can offer both healing to body and mind and insights into our humanity, but we often give brief attention to them. To use our time wisely, we may need to become more aware of these rhythms so that we can more fully under-stand the deeper messages about time which surround us.

The seasons of nature unfold with all their attendant miracles of snowdrops, catkins, bluebells, roses, Michaelmas daisies, falling leaves, and the fine tracery of bare branches silhouetted against a winter sky. The rhythms of the seasons, each with its distinct mood, colour and flavour, are there for us to mark and ponder, if we will but pause and take time to notice, to consider their particular message. When the psalmist 'considers the heavens' and watches the rhythms of the planets and stars, he comes to a deeper understanding of his relationship with God and the wonder of the Creator's involvement with humanity. When Christ invited us to 'consider the ravens' and 'consider the lilies of the fields', it was not just an invitation to indulge in an exercise of nature observation; rather, he used this awareness to prompt us to greater faith and reliance upon God.

Mark pulled the last of the leaves towards him, drag-ging the rake across the grass that was already damp with the early evening mist, and noticed the fading light of the day. The horse chestnut always left a multitude of leaves and it had taken him longer than expected to gather them up. It would soon be time to go in. Kelly had already turned on the lights in the house and he could hear the comforting sounds of cups being clattered and the kettle being filled. The sweet smell of a wood fire came from further down the valley.

Mark loved this season of the year; the gradual turning from the exuberance of bright summer to the mellowness of autumn. He found it fostered a reflective mood within him. It wasn't just that he reviewed the garden, took stock of which plants had flourished, which crops had succeeded, where changes needed to be made. It was more that the falling of the leaves and the shortening of the days had made him think more deeply about the changes in his own life.

He wrestled with a decaying apple caught up in the prongs of the rake and tossed it into the wheelbarrow. There was the starkness of winter to face and a stripping which would leave not only the branches of the trees exposed. He grasped a low branch, bending it towards him, and rubbed his finger along the bough, feeling for the familiar horseshoe-shaped wound from which the leaf had fallen. He smiled. There, even on the bare branch, was a promise of a new leaf and a continuing growth. He hoped the tree would survive the winds and cold of another winter but was alert to its age and the risks of its falling. He wondered if he was prepared for the loss.

The promise of the rhythm of the seasons remains with us:

> While the earth lasts
> Seedtime and harvest, cold and heat,
> Summer and winter, day and night,
> Shall never cease.
>
> (Genesis 8.22 NEB)

As well as the seasonal rhythms, each day brings its own rhythm as the rising and setting of the sun brings a wonderful transformation of the world around us from daybreak to sunset, with subtle changes of darkness and light from the first hint of partial light through to the clarity of midday and then back into the mystery of twilight and the return of night. This daily rhythm brings its own opportunities for reflection and insights.

I used to be afraid of the dark. Not when I was a child. No, then the dark was friendly, epitomized by the gentle drawing of curtains, cosily sitting by the fire watching the sparks on the chimney or lying in the safe darkness of my bedroom hearing the reassuring murmur of conversations in the rooms below.

It was later in life that fear of the dark developed. I first became aware of this on holiday in Tuscany. We stayed at a house kindly loaned to us by a friend. It was remote and reached by an almost inaccessible mountain track. Whilst it had water, cooking was by gas cylinders and light only by candles. In common with most of the houses in the area, the windows had shutters, not curtains, two on the outside and two on the inside. Once in bed with the shutters closed and the candles blown out, the darkness was of a quality I had never experienced before. It was palpable; you could hold it between your fingers like a swathe of velvet and at times it felt as if it would suffocate you. Some nights I felt that the blackness was such that I had in reality lost the power of sight. Terror gripped me and, groping for my shoes, I would creep to the window and open the shutters to catch a reassuring glimpse of the shadowy outlines of trees, or if I was fortunate, the gleaming moon. One night I dreamt I was being put into a coffin and the sense of claustrophobia was overwhelming.

These fears stayed, mainly suppressed, with me until by some grace I found myself back at home praying by the window at twilight. As day's light faded and the colours of the garden gave way to the greys of dusk, I watched the sky gradually change from glorious sunset to deeper indigo to smooth darkness. I watched mesmerized by the beauty of it and then noticed the stars appearing, gradually, one by one, and then more until great galaxies spread across the heavens. There was a moment of sheer gift, for in the fading of the light and the coming of darkness I no longer saw terror but a realization of the interchange between light and dark. The stars had been there all the time, hidden only by the light and limitations of the day. The fading of the light meant not annihilation of life but new worlds, new wonders beyond our wildest imaginings. God created both light and dark: 'Darkness is no darkness to thee and night is luminous as day; to thee both dark and light are one' (Psalm 139.12 NEB).

God created the rhythms of the days and nights as well as the seasons and teaches us about our humanity through them. We each respond in an uniquely individual way and need to discover how the times and the seasons influence our energy, our attitude, our mood. How do the seasons affect us? Are we invigorated by the starkness of winter, or saddened by the stripped branches? Are we cheered by the spring or do we find its vibrancy too overwhelming? Do we enjoy the hot days of summer or prefer the cooler temperatures and muted colours of autumn? Are we a morning person, swift to get up and irritated by those who stay in bed, or do we not really surface until midday and work best when everyone else is asleep? Natural rhythms affect us and if we are to use our time effectively we would do well to listen to how we respond, to learn the lessons freely available around us.

As well as the rhythms evident in nature, God gives us both by example and precept a strong insistence on the importance of the rhythms between work and rest, activity and withdrawal for reflection. In Genesis 2.2 we read: 'On the sixth day God completed all the work he had been doing, and on the seventh day he ceased from all his work. God blessed the seventh day and made it holy, because on that day he ceased from all the work he had set himself to do' (NEB). In the RSV translation the word 'ceased' is translated as 'rested'. Perhaps it is worth pondering whether God still left an 'in tray' of projects for another creative period. The phrases 'completed all the work he had been doing' and 'ceased from all the work he had set himself to do' surely do not necessarily imply that God would not return to the creative task but rather that he saw rest and stopping as an important dimension of the creative process. This emphasis on the balance between rest and activity is echoed very clearly in the commandments received by Moses: 'Remember to keep the Sabbath day holy. You have six days to labour and do all your work. But the seventh day is a Sabbath of the LORD your God' (Exodus 20.8ff. NEB).

Again, in the life of Jesus it would seem that these periods of rest or withdrawal are an essential part of his life rhythm and the vehicle whereby he receives the most significant insights about how to use the time before him. It is during the period in the wilderness that he confronts all the possibilities of how he might live his life and exercise his ministry, following his initial humble offering of himself for baptism by John. We frequently see him taking time apart from his ministry of healing and teaching for periods of withdrawal, solitude and prayer. It is in the lonely isolation of the Garden of Gethsemane that he wrestles with understanding the demands of his calling and then faces the approaching soldiers with both a full realization that 'the hour has come' and a secure assurance of the presence of 'my Father who would at once send to my aid more than twelve thousand legions of angels' (Matthew 26.53–54 NEB).

God's time extends to reveal purposes and plans to us when we least expect it, when we are resting but open to God's voice. In a culture which extols and rewards activity, there is a danger of becoming reliant upon our actions and attributing a self-importance to our deeds. Continual preoccupation with work, whilst often having a very obvious and laudable outcome, can disguise our avoidance of the challenging issues surrounding how we choose to spend our time and how we make decisions about the path of our lives.

If we are serious about recognizing our time as God's time, restoring rhythm to our lives enables us to balance activity with silence, solitude and rest. The stilling of our inward chatter and our outward business gives space for God's Spirit to enter into our time and endow it with the insight of eternity. It allows us to humbly put God at the centre and see activity as a response to God's loving purposes, not as an end in itself. As the Psalmist writes: 'For God alone my soul in silence waits; from him comes my salvation.'

Emma Johnson rested with her class of nine-year-olds outside the Cathedral. They were sharing a drink before the coach journey home to their inner-city school. Secretly she was congratulating herself on how the day had gone. It had been full of purposeful activity and opportunities for learning. The programme had run without a hitch. The children had been fascinated to watch the glaziers and stonemasons at work. They had attended well during the guided tour around the Cathedral and she had been gratified by how much they had remembered of the vocabulary. The words 'cathedra', 'pulpit', 'lectern', 'nave' and 'chancel' had all tripped off their tongues.

She turned to the boy with tousled red curls sitting on the grass beside her. 'Tell me. What have you enjoyed most in the day?'

He fixed her with a steady gaze. 'It was at the end, Miss. When we went into that place at the side and sat down; when we weren't doing anything. I just sat there and looked, and it was so quiet and still and beautiful. It was the silence and the stillness. That was what I liked best.'

Emma looked back towards the spire soaring behind them. She realized that the true purpose of the glorious building behind her had been revealed to this child, regardless of her frenetic activities.

But it is not only balancing activity with rest which is an issue, it is also the risky trust that progress and insight may come when we dare to let go of the reins, disengage our focus and allow another part of our minds some space. Some insights simply come 'out of the blue' and we often solve apparently intractable problems when we 'sleep on it'. It is often when we refrain from active pursuit of a solution that an entirely new, unexpected and not always welcome perspective will 'come to mind'.

Yet in our own culture time spent 'dreaming' is often viewed as slothful or lazy. It is a strange paradox that the twentieth century, a time when the significance of the unconscious and of dreams became the focus of scientific investigation, was also a time when taking regard of dreams and intuition was treated with scepticism and suspicion.

The Bible leaves us in no doubt about the importance of times when we 'sleep on it' and allow ourselves to dream dreams and see visions. In both the Old and New Testaments revelation and guidance is frequently received when people are disengaged from activity and open to God. Moreover, these dreams were in no way an escape into a fantasy world; rather, they were an invitation for people to engage in the challenges which faced them and sometimes to completely revise their mind-set. Joseph, fearing that his betrothal to Mary is ending in ignominy and misery, is reassured and encouraged to pursue his marriage. But he is goaded into swift action to flee to Egypt and into an unexpected and probably unwelcome time as a refugee when a dream foretells the wrath of Herod. Dreams can overturn our preconceived ideas. Ananias argues the toss about going to Saul, pointing out 'all the harm [Saul] has done to thy people in Jerusalem', but the message is clear: 'You must go, for this man is my chosen instrument' (Acts 9.10–19 NEB). Peter's life-long beliefs concerning the cleanliness of certain foods were challenged in his dream which opened his mind to overcome his misgivings about visiting the gentile centurion Cornelius (Acts 10.1–23). For all these people and many more, dreams and visions were not a complete waste of time but rather a time for unexpected revelations, changed perspectives and new insights.

As the members of the committee gathered in the small room of the new village hall, the mood was subdued. The last meeting had ended in an acrimonious argument about the removal of an old dilapidated seat positioned behind the new hall. Since that meeting Maggie, a new member on the committee, had been troubled by a series of recurring dreams. Sometimes they were dreams which awoke her in the night, sometimes just pictures which came into her mind at totally unexpected moments, but they always had a linking image of a person sitting with head in hands. Try as she would, she could not see the face.

She took her place and fiddled with the paper and pen on the table in front of her. A newcomer into the community, she felt too hesitant to share her dream with the others, aware of the suspicion with which such a revelation might be met and how it might discredit her abilities as a cool-headed thinker. But she knew that, however bizarre it might seem, her vision was in some way related to the problem facing them that night.

As the chairperson opened the meeting and the discussion about the seat was about to proceed, an idea came into her mind and she said, 'I wonder if before we start we could each briefly describe how and in what ways the seat is important to us?'

The chairperson visibly sighed and there were some who muttered about wasting time, getting on with decisions, committees were not the place for waffle . . . but eventually the chairperson grudgingly agreed. 'Right! There are twelve of us, so from my left and very briefly, please. What's the seat mean to you?'

The first remarks were terse: 'Not a lot. I never use it.' 'It's always been there, to my knowledge, but I think it's an eyesore now.'

But as the conversation continued, people revealed a little more. 'I have a feeling it was given in memory of someone, but I don't know who. Perhaps we could enquire around?' 'It worries me that it's a health and safety risk and I feel responsible.'

Then some members offered their ideas: 'I often see youngsters sitting there chatting in all weathers. It's made me realize there's nowhere they can congregate safely just for company.' 'Do you realize it's the only place the elderly can sit down when they walk home from the village? They often rest there enjoying the view. Maybe we could offer more at the hall for the elderly?'

The discussion opened out as people revealed their hidden hopes and fears, and Maggie began to see the real faces which had been hidden in the dream.

God does not only speak to us in the times we choose to be attentive. He uses the rhythms of both the day and the night, our times of action and our times of rest and dreaming to unfold his purposes.

Concluding prayer

God of all rhythms
The Creator of day and night, summer and winter, seedtime
    and harvest
Help us to be attentive to the rhythms around us
Calm us with the quiet heartbeat of the seasons
Enlarge our limited vision by the grandeur of your spacious
    purposes
Awaken our ears to the pulse of everyday miracles
Wrap our activity in the calm mantle of your peace
So that freed from compulsion and fear
We may dance in freedom
To the life-giving rhythms of your love.

God of stillness and silence
Who waits for us amidst the noise and clamour of our lives
Whose murmur is heard in quietness
Who whispers through our dreams
Endow us with the courage to rest from activity
Stay with us through the feelings which surface in silence
Strengthen us to listen to instinct and intuition
So that empowered by your presence
We may be free
To behold the visions and dreams you have for our lives.
Amen.

Part 2
Reflections and exercises on Session 3, 'Sensing time's rhythms'

1 Sabbath rest

Scholars tell us that one of the understandings of the word 'sabbath' was 'the day of quieting the heart'. For many people current work patterns make a 'sabbath rest' very difficult.

Take some time to pray for those whose work schedules or responsibilities make a pattern of rest and time for 'quieting the heart' difficult:

- those on shift work;
- those whose work demands flexible and unpredictable hours;
- those who work at nights, at weekends and on public holidays;
- those whose work involves travel and periods of rest apart from family and friends;
- carers of the very young and very old;
- carers of the chronically sick or disabled;
- those without respite from caring.

Take time to look at the pattern of your days and week. How do you protect time for rest and recreation, alone, with family and friends? Are there simple actions you can take to restore a sense of rhythm in your life? For example: putting the phone on answerphone during family meals; designating one evening a week or one meal a week as a relaxed un-hurried time together; taking a quiet walk once a week.

Are there simple actions you could take to support others for whom the rhythm between responsibilities and rest lacks a restorative balance? For example: offering to sit with a young family or an elderly person to give a carer respite; supporting a respite organization financially; speaking out for fair working conditions.

2 Recognizing the times and the seasons

In an exhibition of Monet's work in London great emphasis was placed on the way the artist approached light, often drawing exactly the same scene at different times of the day or in different seasons and marking the changes in colour and tone.

Choose a view from the window or take a walk and notice the different qualities of light which are around you. Notice the effect of the direction and strength of the light on trees and buildings. If possible return to the same view at different times of the day and year. How does the movement of the sun and the season alter the 'feel' of the place? You may choose to paint or write down your observations.

Reflect on how light or the lack of light affects you. Which are the best times of the day for you to work or rest? Which is your favourite season? When do you have most energy? Are there times of the day or seasons which are less effective for you? How can you use this understanding of how you respond to the times and the seasons to help you plan your life, your work and your rest?

3 For everything its season

Read Ecclesiastes 3.1–8. Consider whether, in your own life, you have given yourself time for each season. Have you hurried past events or experiences and not given yourself time to relish or understand their significance for you? Which 'seasons' would it help you to revisit?

The poem below is loosely based on the passage in Ecclesiastes:

For everything its season
And a time for every purpose under heaven:
a time to lie in bed and a time to get up
a time to move and a time to be still
a time to feast and a time to be abstemious
a time to celebrate and a time for serious matters
a time for company and a time for solitude
a time for conversation and a time for sharing silence
a time to concentrate and a time to dream
a time to hasten and a time to slow down

Using the couplet 'For everything its season/And a time for every purpose under heaven' to start, write your own 'time to' poem.

4 A 'savouring the seasons' diary

The pressures of commercialization urge us towards this feeling of being 'behind the times', whipping us towards the next thing before we have savoured the present moment. Christmas cards appear before we have planted the bulbs in the autumn. Hot cross buns and Easter eggs are rapidly becoming detached from any season and available all year round. Children and teachers no sooner skip home for the longed-for summer holidays than the shops place placards proclaiming 'It's back to school'.

Take a small notebook and divide its pages between the twelve months of the year. You could use a diary but one with blank pages would be preferable. At the beginning of each month make a note of what things are special to you this month, what things you usually relish and enjoy. This could be a birthday, the first snowdrops, toasted teacakes by the fire, Christmas decorations in the street, a local carnival, a liturgical season. Each day or week of the month, take a few minutes to give thanks for the particular thing you have noticed, and add others to your list. You may like to paste in photos, postcards, sports programmes or theatre tickets. Be aware of the changing of the time of year in the changing of nature, social life and family events.

5 Noticing the rhythm

Take time to become aware of the rhythms of your body – heartbeat, breathing, the menstrual cycle, the way you walk. Be aware of the rhythm of the music you listen to and how it affects you. How does a march tune, a waltz, a tango or a syncopated rhythm affect your feelings? You may like to explore a new hobby which involves rhythm, dancing, cycling, swimming or aerobics. Consider what fresh insights the awareness of your body and rhythms offers you.

6 Dreams and hunches

Reflect on times in your life when you have had a dream which revealed something important or surprising to you. Have there been times when you have had a hunch about a situation or action which did not seem to correspond to rational analysis but which turned out to be a creative way forward?

SESSION 4

When time stands still

———◆◆◆———

This Session explores:

- experiences of being 'outside time'
- how human ecstasy or desolation affects our perception of time
- how natural beauty and the work of artists, poets or musicians can awaken a different sense of time

Part 1

There are times in our lives when the passing of minutes, hours, days no longer matters and chronological time, time we measure and count, has no relevance or meaning. Children are frequently observed immersed in this different time world, caught up in play or absorbed in watching the slow progress of a snail or delighting in pouring water from one container to another.

> Maggie stood at the edge of the playground sipping her break-time coffee and watching the children as they whirled around her in a hurly-burly of activity. One child caught her eye. He was playing alone and seemed intent upon a galloping game, apparently holding the reins of some imaginary horse. What was at first glance less obvious was the reasoning behind his movements.

He galloped at speed towards a place and then stopped abruptly, his 'horse', it seemed, rearing up as if faced with some obstacle. Sometimes he paused and then jumped with careful attention, watching the ground.

As she followed his changes in direction she suddenly saw a structure governing his movements. A sudden squall of rain prior to playtime had left the asphalt an incredible maze of shapes and patterns. Darker patches marked where it was still wet whilst irregular light shapes had formed on the ground where the rain had dried out. The horseman rode only on the light patches, the wet dark asphalt forming for him a secret world, a land of rivers and mountains, gullies to be negotiated and leaped over, deep gorges where he needed to rein in his horse and avoid a treacherous fall. The child galloped on, oblivious of her attention, in a world of play which had the total concentration of a monk or nun at prayer.

In adulthood we sometimes find it difficult to re-enter the still absorption which is the natural country of young children. Yet there are moments when the passing of time seems immaterial. The experience of falling in love, or of a mature love or deep friendship which has endured, endows ordinary events with a significance and wonder which stand outside time as we usually experience it. Walking hand in hand, sharing a cup of tea inexplicably become joyous moments of sharing and meeting. The ordinary is transformed. As George Herbert put it in 'Prayer (I)', we find 'heaven in ordinarie'.

Tom ran on to the main concourse of Waterloo Station. He thought his meeting would never end and now he was late to meet her train. He scanned the Arrivals screen. The train had arrived on time and ten minutes ago. He hurried anxiously to the platform but Claire was nowhere in sight. Would she have given up on him, wandered off on her own? Would he find her amidst this mêlée of rushing people? He began to panic. She could be anywhere. He knew it was ridiculous. Claire had travelled the world alone and was totally self-reliant, but he suddenly felt gripped by anxiety and felt a rush of protective love as he realized how precious she was to him.

And then, miraculously, he caught sight of her. Her dark hair swinging as she strode towards the newspaper kiosk. He paused, just relishing watching her, her confident walk, her smiling exchange with the assistant, the way she put her head on one side. Just minutes later they had found a seat in the café overlooking the concourse and were sipping coffee.

It was ridiculous, he mused, but he knew he could spend any amount of time caught up in the gaze of her eyes, waiting for the slow smile which erupted into infectious laughter, longing for her to lean forward so he could wind her hair round his finger, touch her face, and steal a kiss. He was oblivious of the surroundings, the other commuters, even the mediocre coffee didn't matter. And as for the insistent announcements of the time of the next train, it suddenly was quite irrelevant.

Human experiences such as falling in love, the joy of sexual delight or the birth of a child can surprise our regimented sensibilities and unexpectedly breach the battlements we make around our hearts. These times of wonder and amazement transport us away from the preoccupation with daily events and tasks and take us to a place where we see time with a completely different perspective. Donne, disturbed from making love by early morning light, chides the sun as 'busy old fool' and 'unruly'. Lovers of every century, caught in the ecstasy and joyous tenderness of love-making, fully understand how their time together is completely beyond any portioning or measurement:

> Love, all alike, no season knows, nor clime,
> Nor hours, days, months, which are the rags of time.

Like the ecstasy of sexual love, seeing your child born into the world can also bring us to the point of recognizing the possibility of miracle once more. It releases us from our mundane and limited expectations into a place where we share in a creative act of such previously unimagined magnitude and mystery – the creation of a separate and distinct, a unique and unknown person. For perhaps a brief moment we inhabit a region beyond our control and governance and recognize the amazing sacred space of life which we so frequently break into measurable fragments to fit our own restricted vision.

It was the silence which she noticed first. After all the pushing and sweating, the mouth-stretching groans and the heart-pumping breathing, that tiny cry of someone else, another being, and then silence as the new life was placed in her arms. She looked down, her hair still clammy and straying across her eyes. Already her child was snuffling and moving towards her, turning to find her breast and moving its so-new mouth to suckle. She could not absorb the otherness of this moment. The tiny ears which had heard only the inner sounds of her body, the limbs confined until now to floating in the waters of her womb. She was mysteriously linked to every woman through the ages who had ever given birth and yet now, in some previously unimagined way, linked to a future, the future of her child and the generations beyond. She felt both part of time and beyond time as she had previously understood it. The present moment was one which would be for ever in her heart and fixed on a date, a 'birth day', but the experience of birth now linked her to a responsibility and a love which was more naturally the stuff of eternity.

Just as experiences of joy or wonder can lift us beyond 'everyday' time, so too can moments of trauma or loss. People who experience traumatic accidents often recall that it was as if time were in slow motion. They could see what was happening but it was unrelated to the speed of ordinary time. The bereaved often describe the time after the death of a relative or friend as feeling like being in a dream, waiting to wake up. One can feel disengaged from the actions one takes, as if walking through mud or on automatic pilot. It is now the ordinary daily activities of others and the usual preoccupations of people and their use of time which seem irrelevant and unimportant. Why are they rushing around to get to work, why don't they stop to talk and enjoy moments together? Can't they see what is really important? When confronted with loss there is a longing for everything to stop, to allow time to recognize the enormity of what has happened and to come to terms with the desolation of spirit.

Peter walked down the flight of steps from the hospital and crossed the road to the bus stop on the further side. It all felt so unreal; the unexpected phone call to his office, the taxi to the hospital, the waiting through the night and now this finality. Even now, though he had watched her breathing to the last, willing each next breath and praying for her to open her eyes just once, he had a compulsive urge to run back to the ward to catch the nurse by the arm and ask, 'Is it true? Is it true?' But grown men don't do that, he sighed. They are meant to deal with the realities of life, whatever that means.

He supposed that 'real life' was what was going on around him. The bus stop was beside a street market. Stalls piled with fruit and vegetables, flower stalls with buckets filled with opening daffodils and vibrantly coloured tulips, clothes stalls with the first of the new spring styles flapping on hangers in the sunshine. And the people laughing and joking, exchanging gossip, buying everyday necessities or indulging themselves or others with unexpected surprises in readiness for the holiday. He watched bemused, bewildered as if behind some glass wall of grief. He no longer felt part of this activity and longed to hold back the inappropriate vitality of spring, to exchange the brightness of the spring day for winter, to put life on hold. He wanted to cry out, 'Don't you know what's happened? She's gone. She's gone. She's gone.' But instead he held out his arm to stop the passing bus, bought an ordinary single fare and stepped on.

At these momentous points in our lives 'ordinary time' seems totally irrelevant and, indeed, an intrusion on the reality of our experienced moment. Sometimes these events are experienced collectively and etched into the memory of a whole community, nation or indeed world. Who cannot remember where they were at the time of the assassination of President Kennedy or the death of Princess Diana? Perhaps the overwhelming response to the death of the famous

is a poignant and public reliving of the common experience
of private loss. Unlike our Victorian forebears, we are urged
to turn back to 'getting on with things' with phrases such as
'life goes on'. Our inner turmoil is no longer signalled to our
community by the wearing of black armbands, or the drawing of curtains. Wonderfully, and sometimes almost despite
the wishes of those who are mourning, life does go on after
bereavement. But the experience of the death of a loved
friend or relative takes time to process and, as bereavement
counsellors will attest, refusing to give time to recognize loss
can lead to later problems and mental health issues.

Judith sat patiently as her client's sobs gradually sub-
sided. She quietly reached out for the ever-present box
of tissues and passed them across the space between
them. This room was not unaccustomed to tears and
as Judith waited for the middle-aged woman to regain
some composure, she reflected on how often the source
of the tears were wells of grief far back in the past
history of the people who sought her help. She gazed
with compassion at the crumpled woman before her
and imagined the scene she had just described. The
drowning of a mother in a freak wave before her eyes;
the snatching of the tiny five-year-old from danger by
bystanders; the coastguard and the ambulance arriving,
and the dreadful unexplained silence. Perhaps, most
significantly, the clumsy attempts at kindness by well-
intentioned relatives who, taking the traumatized child
home, had said, 'We'll take you out to buy a new dress.
That will make you feel better!'

But she hadn't felt better. What she had felt was
an obligation upon her to smile, to pretend everything
was OK, that the fear and confusion in the pit of her

stomach was not there. And so it was that, at the age of sixty-seven, after a lifetime of coping with all manner of trials and tribulations, she found that when her beloved cat died she could not bury grief any more. It all poured out as if the intervening time which had passed was but an interlude waiting for her to stop. The memory of past experiences was not something like old skin which could be sloughed off unnoticed; nor could it, like a childhood milk tooth, be hidden under a pillow, waiting for the tooth fairy to transform it into a shiny sixpence. No, memory demanded the maturity and strength to face realities in real time, to allow time for good grief and then, with courage, to proceed.

Just as extremities of joy or pain can jolt us out of our usual understanding of time, so too beauty in nature, the work of poets and musicians and the wonder of scientific discovery can nudge us towards a deeper reality and a larger vision of time's mysteries, to ponder questions which we usually submerge beneath the daily everyday demands which often dominate our use of time. Most people can recall some incident in their lives when time stopped as they became lost in wonder, whether it was the beauty of a sunset, the magnificence of the pounding waves along a seashore or the flight of an eagle. Sometimes it is the imagination of artists, whether in poetry or dance, music or drama, which challenges us to look again at the world around us. Poets, scientists and composers alike urge us to take time to look again at the miracle of the natural world: the 'fluttering and dancing' of Wordsworth's 'golden daffodils'; Gerard Manley Hopkins's pointing out to us the glory of 'dappled things'; Vaughan Williams's musical evocation of the lark; Rodin's encapsulation of physical love and desire in his sculpture

The Kiss. Their reflections place us in a wider context demanding that we look again at how we perceive our lives. They invite us to stand still for a moment as we absorb more fully the wonder of the present view, the significance of the passing experience, the worth of the casual encounter.

> As she stood by the river she had known as a child, she remembered. It was at this bend of the river that she used to come with her brother when she was small. She fished for tiddlers whilst he sat and painted. They spent hours there, often in silence. For much of the time she was happy enough paddling in and out of the water, trailing her net, putting her catch into the jam jar suspended on a string. When she was bored she used to sit up close to him. She knew he did not like to be watched but if she was quiet sometimes he pointed things out to her. So it was that she learned to watch for the sudden flash of the kingfisher, to be able to distinguish between a coot and a moorhen and to listen for the sudden alarm call which warned of the approach of a water rat. She began to see with new eyes the shades of blue and grey, green and turquoise in the flow of the river, to watch for ripples and flurries of water which announced the presence of larger fish. She would watch spell-bound as the blank paper filled with a new picture, another revelation. 'Anyone can paint,' he used to say. 'You just need to look.' She smiled as she remembered. Such looking, such attentive looking was the gift of artists.

Musicians, poets, artists and scientists invite us to look beyond the immediate and obvious, to reflect on what we see, to think about our relationships, our values, our society and our presuppositions. They invite us to re-enter that place where time stands still so that we may see more clearly the amazing wonder of the 'now' in all its pain, ambiguity, glory and paradox. They also challenge us to look afresh at how we perceive and use time when our senses have been opened to a wider vision and deeper insights. In those time-stopping revelations we link ourselves with the experience of Moses who saw not a scrubby thorn tree but the 'flame of a burning bush' and we put ourselves in the company of the disciples who, on the mountain-top, saw beyond the popular preacher and healer to a transfigured Christ. These 'out of time' moments, whether of joy, pain or wonder, nudge us, like Moses, to take off the shoes of convention, respectability or culture and step beyond the preconceptions of this present time. For whatever reason, time stands still, and we are lifted into a different experience of time – time where we reach towards the transcendent and dare to dream and confront previously unthought-of possibilities and unimagined scenarios. It is an experience of time which reminds us, in the words of Emily Dickinson, that:

> This world is not Conclusion.
> A Species stands beyond.

Concluding prayer

Mysterious God
You enter into our lives in joy and sorrow
In ecstasy and desolation
You reveal yourself
In the fragile song of the bird
The mighty thunder of the sea
The quiet beauty of an opening flower
The majesty of mountains
And the wonder of a newborn child.

Help us to hold fast to those moments of transfiguration
To carry the insights we are given into the toil of everyday
  time
To nurture the wisdom of eternity amidst the demands of
  today.
Amen.

Part 2
Reflections and exercises on Session 4, 'When time stands still'

1 When time stood still

Bring to mind an event in your life when time stood still for you, whether it was falling in love, a birth, a death, a joyful or a traumatic event.

Allow yourself time to recall where you were, who was with you, what happened, how you felt.

How were your values and expectations changed by the event?

Were there things which seemed clearer at that time than when you are immersed in humdrum everyday life?

Did time matter and, if so, in what ways?

Are there insights which occurred during these periods which you want to incorporate into your daily use of time? Make a list of your conclusions under the heading: 'These things I know about time'.

2 Becoming as a child

As we leave childhood behind we can mistakenly feel that 'playing' is not a permitted use of time for adults!

Look at the pattern of your life today. How do you make time for relaxation and absorbing yourself in an interest or hobby?

Is there something you have always wanted to do but never made time for?

The writer Mary Wesley's first novel was published when she was seventy years of age. A friend of mine started to learn to tap dance in her sixties!

Have you allowed time to go by without allowing for creative play?

Can you organize your responsibilities in such a way as to allow time for 'play'?

3 The inward eye

Wordsworth speaks of how often he returned to the sight of the daffodils and how they affected his spirits.

Choose a piece of music or a poem.

Allow yourself simply to enter into the mood of the music or to envisage the scene depicted in the poem. Identify a phrase from the poem or a passage from the music which you can return to for refreshment during 'everyday' time.

You may like to make a collection of these 'mantras' which can remind you of 'still time' when you are busy or stressed.

4 Walking out of time

Plan a route for a walk which is fairly familiar and so won't involve map reading or anxiety about the time it will take. Give yourself permission to 'stand and stare' rather than keeping moving. Be gently aware of all that you see, hear and touch during the walk. Pause to touch the bark of trees, observe the different shapes and shades of leaves, notice the near and far views. Stand still to listen to the sounds of people, birds, animals and machines. Use all your senses of sight, touch, hearing and smell to enjoy the surroundings.

5 A childhood vision

In his book *Journey from Obscurity*,[5] Harold Owen recalls an event from childhood. He describes walking home from Evensong across buttercup-filled fields with his brother Wilfred, who later became a renowned war poet. Climbing over a stile, Harold noticed that the petals of the buttercups had clung to his boots, giving them a mysterious golden glow which the brothers marvelled at together. Recalling this as an adult, he remarks on the experience of spirituality he enjoyed during those childhood walks.

Take time to recall things which you enjoyed as a child and which gave you cause for wonder, or, if you prefer, think of something a child has shown you with wonder. How did these times of looking and wondering lift you beyond ordinary time? Is there something you have noticed recently which lifted you out of time?

SESSION 5

The time of your lives

———⬥◆⬥———

This Session explores:

- our awareness of the historical period within which we live
- how the events of our lifetime might have affected us
- how inventions and social changes might influence our expectations and values

Part 1

In his famous speech in *As You Like It* Jaques describes what has become known as the 'seven ages' of life, beginning with 'the infant mewling and puking in the nurse's arms' and tracing the time of life through childhood, adolescence, adulthood until:

> [The] last scene of all that ends this strange eventful
> history,
> Is second childishness, and mere oblivion,
> Sans teeth, sans eyes, sans taste, sans everything.

This 'strange eventful history' sometimes seems to proceed so imperceptibly that we hardly notice its inevitable march. Inscribed inside the door of a grandfather clock in Chester Cathedral was this verse:

When, as a child, I laughed and wept
Time crept.
When, as a youth, I dreamed and talked
Time walked.
When I became a full grown man,
Time ran
And later, as I older grew,
Time flew.
Soon I shall find, while travelling on,
Time gone.
Will Christ have saved my soul
By then?
Amen.[6]

Many of us can identify with the father in the musical *Fiddler on the Roof* who muses as he attends his daughter's wedding. He wonders at the passing of days and years he cannot remember and sees with incredulity that the children he once carried in his arms are now fully grown, independent adults. Yet, whether we notice it or not, as we live through the time of our lives we experience considerable changes, some more obvious than others. Our early years are marked by immense and very noticeable developments. The progression of an infant from birth to the age of one is an incredible journey, and the subsequent changes of a child from one to five, as they acquire the ability to feed themselves, walk, speak and master a range of social, motor and intellectual skills, are an everyday miracle which often goes unnoticed, except by the rather inadequate exclamation, 'How they have grown!'

Parents of teenagers will not be unaware of the alterations time brings on an almost daily basis as their offspring develop physically and also test out their growing independence and autonomy. But as we enter adulthood these physical differences are less dramatic. Who could reliably tell whether a young man was twenty-seven or thirty-three? Who would dare to accurately gauge whether a woman was forty-five or fifty-two? In the Western world, better health care and increased opportunities for a good diet and healthy lifestyle have extended the time in which people can engage in an active life. Only gradually do the restrictions of an ageing body become visible, and many are spared the 'sans everything' experience. Eighty has become the new sixty, as a recent newspaper headline proclaimed.

But the time of our lives is not just concerned with our physical changes through time. We have all been affected by the historical period during which we happen to have been born and nurtured. Sometimes we do not pause to recognize how the historical and social events of our lifetime have affected us and influenced the people we become and our attitudes towards how we experience time.

The family had gathered from near and far to celebrate Aunt May's ninetieth birthday. She still lived in the house in which she had been born and which her parents had moved into during their early married years. However, today her family had not only travelled from all over the country to be with her, but from all over the world: a grandson who now worked in Brussels and a granddaughter who had married an Australian she met whilst backpacking.

The only 'backpack' May had known was the kit bag she had seen her father bring back from the First World War. She had experienced two world wars, lived through the days of the Depression and the General Strike and watched as the tiny rural village where she grew up developed into a noisy commuter suburb.

As a young woman she had nearly died with rheumatic fever and the family had considered themselves blessed as the local doctor did not charge for all of his frequent visits. During her lifetime penicillin and antibiotics had become commonplace and free medical care alongside free education an expected right.

Brought up in a tiny village where walking to the market town seven miles away was an adventure, she had watched the advent of the car, the plane and space travel. As a child the boys had played cricket in the road and she had been free to wander at will in the meadows behind her house. Now traffic made the road too dangerous for children to cross alone and unaccompanied walks had been considered inadvisable for her own grandchildren.

Whilst her entertainment had been around a family piano or a dance at a local hall, she had firstly enjoyed radio, then cinema, and bought a television to watch the coronation of Elizabeth II. She hadn't yet mastered a computer or surfing the web – commonplace things for the younger members of her family. Her present back pain may have been in part started by the use of a heavy hand-mangle for washing, but she now had a washing machine in her kitchen and a freezer full of vegetables she would have previously grown herself whilst 'digging for victory'.

As she held her great-granddaughter in her arms, she marvelled at the different life this child would have. Her granddaughter was well on the way to becoming a successful career woman, and this child would grow up with very different understandings and expectations. What changes would the time of her life contain?

We are often so preoccupied with the everyday that whilst we observe the momentous events which happen in the world and note the changes going on, we only occasionally take stock of how living through this particular period of history has affected us. Whether we recognize it or not, we have all been forged within the historical context of our lives and the events on the world stage will have affected our outlook and attitudes. The war memorials in villages and towns throughout the land bear the names of people who were known and loved in those communities. Most people growing up during the Second World War personally knew someone who had died or been maimed. Many had witnessed the bombing of cities at first hand or had listened to the stories of people who had. For many in Britain today, experience of war is through television coverage and the news media. Pictures of devastation and famine from around the globe are commonplace, but in Britain only a minority have experienced this at first hand. What difference does seeing images of war rather than knowing war on a personal level make to our perceptions of war and conflict? Has it made us more compassionate or do we have more information but less understanding?

Rosemary stood at the War Memorial and the last notes of the trumpet faded across the surrounding fields. She glanced around her at the still bowed heads of the village community. So few left now who remembered the Second World War. She had been a child living in a different place from this, a village just north of London. Many village families had evacuees staying. Her family had been lucky. They had room to grow their own vegetables and keep chickens, so she was never hungry and they shared food with neighbours.

But she mused now at how living through that time had affected her. Even now she could not break an egg open without scraping out the last scrap of white from the shell; she seldom threw anything away, a piece of string, a carrier bag, a 'useful' tin. She had a 'make-do and mend' mentality; 'left-over' food was still resurrected into some kind of meal whilst her grandchildren smiled at her for bothering to mend her tights.

But as she turned to walk quietly away from the churchyard she realized that the effects of living through that time had gone deeper than residual frugality. She remembered nights spent in the shelter and the sound of distant thudding as London was bombed. And then there were the times they had watched as the planes from the nearby aerodrome had droned overhead. She recalled her grandmother looking up at the sky dark with planes and sobbing: 'God bless you, boys. Come back safely.' It was the only time she had seen her grandmother cry. Generally the women around her had taken on the extra burdens and loneliness of wartime with a courage epitomized by the dogged optimism of the songs they sang whilst working: 'There'll be bluebirds over the white cliffs of Dover'; 'Smile though your heart is breaking'.

Surrounded by the loss and pain of others – a neighbour whose three sons had been killed, an uncle maimed for life by the loss of his legs – Rosemary had learned to cover her own needs, to disguise the lesser trials of childhood and growing up. Just being alive was enough cause for gratitude; to wake to another day was cause for rejoicing. Yet, even now she had only to hear the wail of a siren to feel the knot of sick anxiety in

her stomach, to remember and wonder what a childhood lived without fear would have been like.

It is not only events, but also the attitudes and values of the
historical time within which we live which can influence our
outlook and the way we use the time of our lives. In 2004
the amount of personal loan in Britain exceeded the trillion-
pound mark. This 'credit-card culture' would have been
seen as a sign of deep disgrace by those living in the first half
of the twentieth century, who would have called credit 'debt'
and whose habit of 'saving for a rainy day' was ingrained by
living through years when unemployment was not cushioned
by a state benefits system. The possibility of purchasing
something without some security is a relatively new phe-
nomenon and has 'taken the waiting out of wanting', as the
first hire-purchase loans bragged.

But how has this development affected the way we spend
our time? How has this relatively easy availability of credit
affected the choices we make about time? Has the 'work
culture', the need to work longer to service debt and the
development of shopping as a leisure pursuit, eroded our
'free' time?

The scientific and medical discoveries which occur during
the time of our lives also impinge on who we become and
the choices we make for our lives. A chemist's shop in the
1960s would have had a single shelf of painkillers, perhaps aspirin or paracetamol. Today any chemist has a range
of drugs for pain control, from migraine to back pain or
symptoms of flu. The production and consumption of painkillers has increased phenomenally. Advertisements on
TV urge us to reach for a tablet at the onset of pain to ensure
that pain does not prevent us from getting on with either

work or leisure pursuits. Pain is seen as a nuisance, an inter-ference which must be rapidly overcome and eliminated.

But there is another view of pain. In the book *Pain: The Gift Nobody Wants* Paul Brand and Philip Yancey write of their work amongst leprosy patients. Leprosy is a disease which attacks the nerves under the skin, leading to loss of feeling. This inability to feel and to recognize pain results in injuries to limbs, damage of which the leprosy sufferer is completely unaware. Without the 'gift' of pain, leprosy suffer-ers can burn or cut themselves or walk on dislocated joints, causing sometimes irreversible damage to their bodies. For leprosy sufferers the absence of pain leaves them in danger.

Anyone who has coped with debilitating pain or witnessed someone they love suffering agony would applaud all efforts to relieve pain. There is no intrinsic merit in pain. However, do we need to recognize that sometimes the presence of pain is a helpful indicator that we need to take responsible action to care for our bodies? We are perhaps encouraged today to always see pain as an enemy; indeed, advertisements sometimes depict pain as a devil or an attacking animal. But could pain sometimes be a warning to reassess the way we spend our time? Is the pain of continual headaches or stress a comment on our work/life balance? Is our aching back a reminder that we need to spend more time walking and less hunched in a car? Are there some life lessons which we only confront and learn when we are faced with pain?

Alongside the escalation of drug consumption to deal with physical conditions, another drug use has developed: so-called 'recreational drugs', drugs to disguise and mask the pain of being human. Those times when we feel lonely, a failure, isolated, without energy, or simply in need of 'a lift', can ostensibly be assuaged by the purchase of mind-altering drugs with a variety of results and consequences.

How has this availability of drugs changed our expectations of everyday experience? Do we expect life to be pain free on both the physical and emotional levels? Just as we may resent spending time in our life on rest and allowing the healing processes of the body to work, are we unwilling as a community to spend time in our lives listening to each other and supporting the anxious or needy through the inevitable difficulties of life, before they become seemingly insurmountable emotional problems? How has the advent of drugs, legal or illegal, affected the time of your life?

Living through the twentieth and early twenty-first centuries has particularly affected the opportunities and choices for women. The advent of freely available contraceptive advice, the development of the Pill, and the rise of feminism have irrevocably altered the way women can use their time. Women suddenly had choice about whether or not to conceive, whether and when to spend time raising a family, and how many children they might have. The changes for women which followed, the greater opportunities for career development and financial independence, and the gradual changes in how men and women balance time for work and family, continue to reverberate around social and political decisions.

'But why have you decided to turn the promotion down?' Mary challenged her daughter across the kitchen table.

'It would be too much travelling. I would be away from home so much,' Lucy replied.

'But you've got a nanny. Ben adores her. Anita is brilliant with him. And it's not as if Sam isn't a supportive husband. He's always encouraged you to get beyond the ceiling. You've always loved travelling.'

71

Lucy sighed. 'But it's not what I want any more. I know this may sound silly to you, Mum, but we're thinking of changing our lifestyle, perhaps even moving.'

'Moving from this lovely house? Why? It's ideal: easy for the airport, big enough for Anita to have a room, a playgroup and school nearby for later on.'

'Please listen. I know it must sound such an un-believable opportunity to you, but what I want is time, time to spend with Ben, with Sam, perhaps to have another baby, to be at home a bit more. Perhaps to work part time or freelance. All these other perks, the promotion, the extra money, suddenly seem less attract-ive, even immaterial.'

'Well, think it over, at least,' said Mary as she picked up her bag and briefcase. Driving home, she pondered the irony of it all. She had spent her life fighting for women's rights in the workplace, encouraging her daughters to take every opportunity which came their way, to refuse to be pigeon-holed, to stand up against sexual discrimination. Now here was her own daughter perhaps choosing to give it all up, to return to being an apple-pie mother, to spend her time at home.

Mary thought about her own life, the choices she had made and her lack of choice. Childcare had only been available for the very rich; maternity leave had simply been time off during later pregnancy before women left the world of work for the world of being a housewife and mother. Men's roles as fathers were hardly in the equation at all.

How had all this affected her relationships, her mar-riage, her family, her sense of self-worth? And how were all the present changes in work pressures, the culture of 24/7 working hours and the aspirations of this generation affecting her daughter? Perhaps times were changing yet again.

We need to consider not only the many social, political and cultural changes that we experience during the time of our lives, but also the speed at which these changes have taken place over the last century. Whilst in another generation patience might have been seen as a virtue, waiting for anything is now seen as a hindrance and necessarily bad. We demand that our transport is unfailingly on time, even if such insistence might sometimes lead workers under pressure to overlook necessary checking and safety procedures. We want our leaders to make instant comment on unfolding news when sometimes to reflect on events might be the wiser course. The opening of worldwide travel, the technological revolution and the speed of modern communication have resulted in very different life experiences. To fly from one side of the world to the other, to have a telephone conference with people on different continents, to watch world events even as they happen, are seen as commonplace things, yet they all affect our attitude towards time, since with these wonderful developments have come new demands and expectations. Whilst previously families may have lived rather similar lives for generation after generation, today's young people are experiencing a completely different world from that of their parents or grandparents.

Will walked into the departure lounge and turned one last time to wave to his father. He watched as his familiar shape disappeared into the crowds on the main concourse of the airport. He looked at his watch. Another hour before his flight was due to leave. With so much security, they had had to be at the airport very early. He would find himself a coffee and perhaps look through the documents for the meeting again.

Strange, he thought, as he made his way towards a free table, that he should be going to New York at much the same age as his father had some forty years earlier; but in very different circumstances.

As they enjoyed a farewell family meal together on the previous evening, his parents had, unusually, shared their memories of the early years of their marriage. His father, David, had gone to New York as a post-graduate on a university scholarship. Unbelievable as it seemed now, flying was then an impossibly expensive luxury, and instead David had enjoyed a week on the *Queen Elizabeth*. Communications with Sally, Will's mother, had been only by letter for a whole year, as then transatlantic telephone calls had to be booked in advance and were both expensive and unreliable.

Will could not imagine his firm allowing him a week to get to a meeting. He regularly flew to different destinations around Europe and North America, and although this contract was for six months, he could easily pop back if necessary. As for only communicating with his partner Isobel by letter – he just could not conceive of it. He would phone or text her as soon as he arrived and he knew there would be an email on his laptop from her.

He smiled as he remembered his father's descriptions of doing research and how the following years of his work had involved trying to access papers, attend international conferences and make contact with others in his field. Whilst for David plans had to be typed out, laboriously copied and then sent by post, for Will it was a different ball game. He often arranged a whole conference in twenty-four hours, accessing information on the internet and contacting colleagues across the world by email.

Will finished his coffee and opened his laptop. He would send his mother a 'Thank you' card for the meal last night. He wondered if she would be able to work out how to open the attachment.

Whether we notice it or not, we will have been radically affected by the economic and political mood of the time, the medical and technical advances and the historical events unfolding on the world stage. It is worth reflecting on how all these influences have impinged on the way we spend our time, how we value our lives and our expectations about whom we might become. Whether we were a 'war baby' or a 'Thatcher child', we live within an historical framework which has undoubtedly coloured how we view the time of our lives.

Concluding prayer

God of the ages
We lay before you the time of our lives
The political events which have influenced our outlook
The educational experiences which have moulded our attitudes
The prevailing culture which has shaped our values.
Help us to be aware of the time of our lives
Astute in our perceptions
Discriminating in our choices
Wise in our judgements
Merciful in our actions
Walking in your presence all the time of our lives.
Amen.

Part 2
Reflections and exercises on Session 5, 'The time of your lives'

1 As time goes by

Using the following headings to help focus your reflections, make a list of the major events and changes which have occurred during your lifetime.

- Medical provision and advances
- Social changes, housing, welfare benefits, class divisions
- Varieties of communications, e.g. post, telephone, email
- Employment, working practices and work/life balance
- Schools and universities, educational provision and style
- Money, wealth and poverty
- Gender, women's emancipation and expectations
- Politics, governments and world events

2 His story, her story

Using your 'As time goes by' list, take one aspect or event of social or political history in your lifetime – e.g. a medical advance, working practices, women's emancipation, the development of household goods, computer access.

How has this affected your life and attitudes? What advantages have there been? Are there any disadvantages? How has this event or invention affected your underlying values? How has it affected your outlook? Are their values which have developed in society which are counter to your spiritual beliefs or moral values?

3 The generation game

Think of a friend or family member who is either in the generation before you or in the one after you. Take time to remember the time of their life. What events have they lived through? What has changed in their lifetime?

How is your life different? How has this altered your perceptions on life? How are your value systems different? How does this affect relationships with the older or younger generation?

4 'They're playing your tune'

Make a list of the songs, tunes or pieces of music which have been important during your life. Which tunes influenced you? What memories of your life do they evoke? If possible, listen to some of the music and allow yourself to enter into the feelings of that time of your life.

What does your choice of tunes reveal about the period you regard as the 'time of your life'? What do you know of the tunes of other generations or communities?

5 Time search

Use a search engine and the many historical websites available to find images and comments on the historical period during which you have lived. You may like to key in words or dates connected with an influential period of your life and see what emerges. Using these and your own resources, you may choose to make a collage of your findings in order to express what is most significant in the time of *your* life.

SESSION 6

This is the day

This Session explores the challenge of seeing God in the present moment of time by looking at:

- the place of forgiveness in living 'now'
- the 'Kingdom' possibilities of all circumstances
- our responsibility for our everyday choices

Part 1

'The time has come, the kingdom of God is upon you.' There is an urgency at the opening of the Gospel of St Mark: the command to 'prepare a way for the Lord'; John's ministry and call to repentance; the swift entrance of Jesus; his baptism; his time in the wilderness. All these things are covered in a mere thirteen verses, and then in the fourteenth verse we have news of John's arrest and Jesus arriving in Galilee with the startling words, 'The time has come, the kingdom of God is upon you' (Mark 1.14 NEB). There is a breathless momentum to Christ's mission: the call of the disciples, on to Capernaum, preaching in the synagogue, healing the sick, all follow in rapid succession. And when the disciples search out Jesus already at prayer early in the morning, his response is not to return to those who already clamour for his presence but to move on 'to the country towns in the neighbourhood: I have to proclaim my message there also.' There is an energy, a vitality, a reaching out to inhabit the present moment with purpose: 'that is what I came out to do' (Mark 1.38 NEB).

This challenge of the present is reflected in St Paul's words to the Romans: 'In all this remember how critical the moment is. It is time for you to wake out of sleep, for deliverance is nearer to us now than it was when first we believed. It is far on in the night; day is near' (Romans 13.11 NEB). Again there is the demand that we see the importance of the now, the significance of the present moment.

But when is this 'now'? The elusive nature and mystery of the present can taunt us. The 'now' is continually changing from being the future into becoming the past; the present is caught in a continual flux. Who has not at times felt that there is an inevitability about the march of time, a hopelessness that we are but pawns in a relentlessly moving catalogue of events, caught between a past which we cannot change and a future over which we may have little control, and through which we may experience only transitory joy.

What does it mean to be a finite human who has a beginning and an end? How do we find meaning when we are daily reminded of mortality, whether in the subtle decay of a fallen apple or the violent deaths in a terrorist attack portrayed on our television screens? 'Time, like an ever-rolling stream, bears all its sons away' can suggest that there is a futility, a vanity about a life which may end 'forgotten, as a dream'.

Yet it is this 'now' which is our life. We have a space of time between our birth and our death, and how we choose to measure, use and value it will both reflect and determine whether we feel that it signifies nothing or everything.

So how do we respond to the call that this very day is the day, the moment of God's Kingdom? Three small steps towards seeing that 'this is the day' could be: to see the place of forgiveness as a tool to enable us to live the present moment more fully; to be willing to recognize the 'Kingdom' possibilities of all circumstances; and to develop a sense of responsibility for our everyday choices, whether large or small.

To live as if 'this is the day' requires that we let go of those things which drag us into the past. Our past can sometimes be a blessing but also sometimes a heavy burden which prevents us moving on. This does not mean ignoring the significance of our history and how it has affected us. Rather it is about reconciling ourselves with this past, making peace with what has been and forgiving ourselves and others. Only in the giving and receiving of this liberating forgiveness can we freely inhabit the present and travel into the future. Individuals and nations who have experienced trauma, brutality, discrimination or rejection may struggle daily for the grace and generosity to forgive or to accept forgiveness.

Forgiving and being forgiven is a complex journey which demands a humility and searing honesty which may not be accomplished overnight. To the baptismal question, 'Do you turn to Christ?' we may sometimes want to reply, 'Would a half turn do?' To face Christ as a penitent demands facing change. Often we prefer to clatter about in past chains rather than live the 'now' of Christ's penetrating gaze. To truly hear the radical words, 'Forgive us as we forgive those who trespass against us' is to hear a wake-up call that many of us would rather sleep through. The compassionate invitation of Christ to live as forgiven and restored people is as challenging today as it was to the adulteress who encountered Christ two millennia ago.

Now back at home she lay alone
Reflecting on the day just past
The brutal entrance of the guards
The lover's ignominious flight
Naked, and privacy exposed
The shouts and slurs, 'Adulteress!'
What did they know of what had been?
Her past, her present, all her pain
The coldness of her husband's bed
The lure of coins for bread and oil

Standing she had endured their gaze
Humiliated stood her ground
Watched as they chose their stone to hurl
Waited as they debated sin
And then the writing in the sand
'I don't condemn you. Sin no more'
Compassion and forgiveness meet
The chance of one more open door

And now, released, she lay alone
Spared from cruel stoning, true enough
But freedom's balm is costlier stuff
A metamorphosis of heart
A willingness to bless the past
A turning from the sins that cling
The memories that haunt our dreams
More terrifying still the call
To live the present uncondemned

It can be hard to live in the present and sometimes we find offering forgiveness or, indeed, perhaps the humility of accepting forgiveness more than we can deal with, and we choose instead to track back yet again over past mistakes and regrets.

It is as if we need to have a 'Past Anonymous', an organization to which we can appeal when we find ourselves sipping the tempting potion of destructive living in the past. We sometimes find that to continue with lifestyles and attitudes which are familiar is a comfort, however stifling and limiting the routine.

> Sweeping the kitchen floor one day, Pat discovered a tiny spider amidst the crumbs and dust. She tried to gently disentangle it and pick it up in order to put it into the freedom and light of the garden. But the spider resolutely scurried back into the corner of the dustpan, crouching and playing dead. How like myself, she mused – unable to recognize God's desire for my fullness of life, the chances for freedom. How often I have turned away from the opportunity of the moment, preferring to stay within the safe confines of my chosen prison.

The author of the Epistle to the Hebrews writes: 'we must throw off every encumbrance, every sin to which we cling, and run with resolution the race for which we are entered' (Hebrews 12.1 NEB). Perhaps this means that we have to focus on the 'now race' and not hanker after other events for which we wish we had qualified, or other races which we spoiled by contravening the drugs regulations! A runner who continually looks over the shoulder risks both losing speed and tripping up on unseen hazards. To live 'now' requires a fundamental turning of the heart.

To see that 'this is the day' also requires the gift of recognition, the ability to discern the sometimes unexpected and perhaps unwanted possibilities of each present moment. Per-haps our greatest loss may be not to recognize the 'now' at all and to pass through whole sequences of life in a dream-like quality of existence, not so much 'as if there were no tomorrow' but as if 'today' did not exist or have a reality of its own.

We can sometimes behave as if our real life begins in the future. A 'when I have done this' scenario emerges. When I have passed my exams, qualified, got married, when the children are older, when I have cleared my debts, when my back is better, when there is less pressure at work, and so on. Our life does not begin when we have achieved the pinnacle of our career, met all our targets, received the accolades of our contemporaries, nor even when we have accomplished all the housework and the ironing is tidily packed away.

The Kingdom of Heaven is not some futuristic haven of perfection but is something for us to experience today in the working out of our everyday time. We experience the Kingdom within the messiness and unexpected traumas of our lives. This recognition of the Kingdom quality of the present moment requires a certain humility in the way we judge what is or is not of ultimate value. It is not only that we are sometimes keen to pass over and hurry through the ordinary events of time in order to get on to the 'important' task, but also that we may divide our lives into 'good times' and 'bad times', perhaps seeing times of sadness, difficulty or disappointment as periods of wasted time and lost opportunity.

Yet, if God is in all our time, God must surely be working through all these moments, whether they appear insignificant, boring, distressing or even destructive. God, through the person of Christ, identifies with joy and pain, success and failure, hope and fear, love and hate, our beginning and our ending. God's creative and redemptive love lifts all our time into a wholeness where nothing is lost and all is finally and wonderfully completed.

Christ warns us about the danger of not recognizing the time of our lives. He mocks his listeners for being able to tell the weather by observing the patterns of the clouds and the wind, but not reflecting upon the time and events they are living through or recognizing their importance (Luke 12.54–6). The parable of the great feast shows a host who is furious that the people he has invited are so preoccupied with their daily concerns about work, finances and relationships that they do not recognize the significance of the invitation or the opportunity of the present moment (Luke 14.15–24). The parable of the ten girls with their lamps (Matthew 25.1–13) alerts us to the necessity of being awake to the needs and demands of the moment, whilst the story of Dives and Lazarus shows the immense regret of the rich man who too late realizes what his life was meant to be about (Luke 16.19–31). Chillingly, the words of Abraham in the story warn of the human unwillingness to see the eternal priorities of the 'now': 'they will pay no heed even if someone were to rise from death'.

This was not what she had planned. Leaning against the kitchen units, she had managed to make a cup of coffee but now realized there was no way she could carry it into the living-room while balancing on crutches.

She looked at her watch. The plane would just be taking off. The holiday had been a year in the planning. She was meant to be with them all, jetting away to sun and snow and a week of ski-ing. Frustration and a sneaking self-pity arose within her. If only she hadn't tried to run for the train, caught her heel in the escalator, wrenched her ankle.

She finished her coffee, hobbled to a more comfortable chair in a different room and surveyed the scene. She had never spent a whole week alone at home, nor had she experienced immobility before. She had been told that in Chinese the word for 'crisis' is the same as the word for 'opportunity'. She heaved a sigh. What opportunities could there possibly be in this set-up of disappointed hopes and broken dreams?

Lying back, she glanced at the room around her. She loved this house, she reflected, and as she looked more carefully she recognized that it was full of love. There was the evidence of her own care as she had built up a home where she and others could rest and enjoy company, but there was something more. As she looked she discovered that the room was full of gifts from other people. There was a painting of her childhood church done by her brother, reminding her of her family and all they had done to cherish and support her vocation. Hanging alongside was a print of the cathedral where she had worked, given as a gift from much-loved colleagues when she moved from the job.

She spent time allowing her eyes to rest on paintings, books, ornaments and vases. Each one had a tale to tell: a tiny glass candle-holder from a dear friend; a silver box given to her on the eve of her wedding by a penurious widow; a paperweight she had purchased at the end of an amazing pilgrimage.

She began to relax, to wipe tears not of frustration but of gratitude as she recognized and acknowledged all the friendship and love which had accompanied her throughout her life. Perhaps this pause was time to be thankful, to get in touch with friends again, to rest in stillness and to find a different kind of holy day.

It is easy to understand why we are tempted to view the disappointments and sorrows of our lives as times when our use of time is interrupted and wastes away. We sometimes dismiss times of enforced waiting, regarding them as annoying delays to our cherished plans rather than as God-given times for reflection or reassessing our lives. Similarly, when our hopes are dashed and our dreams broken, it is extremely hard to recognize the bottom of the pit as the place where the Kingdom of God might grow and even flourish. When Jacob was alone at Mahaneh, the story tells us of how he wrestled with the man until daybreak and until the man gave Jacob his blessing (Genesis 32.24–32). Whether it is illness, bereavement in all its many forms, betrayal or the challenge of our own mortality, we are entrusted with the task of wrestling until the dawn, of struggling to discover blessings, to nurture the Kingdom in the present moment of our circumstances, however unprepossessing they may be. It may help us to remember that the 'now' of the unfolding flower of 'Kingdom time' was present in the tears of the heart-broken Peter, in the hesitant walk of the women visiting the tomb while it was yet dark, in the disciples who gathered, still afraid, in the upper room, in the questioning and doubts of the friends on the Emmaus road. It is this today in all its complexity and ambiguity – its injustices, anxieties, disappointments and fears – within which the Kingdom will be manifest.

To live now also requires that we accept responsibility for our present choices, and recognize the significance of each choice we make. Writing about the character of Judas, Brother Ramon points out that whereas in St Matthew's Gospel Judas is described as 'Judas Iscariot the man who betrayed him [Jesus]' (Matthew 10.4), St Luke speaks of 'Judas Iscariot who *became* a traitor' (Luke 6.16).[7] In the chapter on Judas and the events of Holy Week, Brother Ramon explores the possibilities and choices which may have confronted Judas on his way to the point where he chose to betray Christ. He points out how 'becoming' is the result of a gradual process of actions and decisions.

We too are 'becoming' people, men and women and children whose daily lives and decisions, small and large, influence the 'now' and the future, and are inevitably linked to past times. So often we are aware of the larger decisions of our lives but give little thought to the underlying attitudes and values which underpin our daily behaviour and that of our societies and communities. Our small decisions also influence our lives and those of others for better or worse.

Living in the now requires an attention to every decision, seeing our everyday actions and decisions as a step towards or against the building of the Kingdom: how we speak to those we meet on a daily basis; the work we choose to do; how we choose to spend our money; the use of our power as consumers; our political decisions; our action in our local community; the television programmes we watch; the attitudes we take to disappointment and failure; indeed, both how we spend all our time and the choices we enable others to have. Living as if 'this is the day' requires a commitment to choosing life-giving options. It means being alert to how these choices affect us, and constantly vigilant about how our exercising of our choice may enhance or diminish the lives of others.

Moses, speaking to the people of Israel about the gift of the commandments, says: 'Today . . . I offer you the choice of life or death, blessing or curse. Choose life and then you and your descendants will live' (Deuteronomy 30.19 NEB). In living 'now' we need to respect our every moment, to give it worth, to recognize that, whatever we are engaged in, it involves a choice in our 'becoming' and as such contributes towards life or death. Whether the choice is small or large, it can influence us and others.

Sarah saved the document she had finished and stretched; time to have a break from the screen. She walked towards the coffee machine in the centre of the office where two of her colleagues were already gathering.

'So, did you see her getting into his car, then?' Cathy was asking Julia.

'Well . . .' Julia hesitated. 'I didn't actually see that, but they did walk out of the office together and were laughing about something as if they were sharing a plan.'

'What a swine! And his wife is expecting their first baby! You know, we've collected quite a bit for a present. I don't know how they could do it – do you, Sarah?'

'Do what?' Sarah hedged for time. She was well aware of the office gossip about Dilly and Mike, but she had also known Dilly for a long time; she was kind and reliable, always interested in others and their concerns.

Sarah was also aware how office gossip had once ruined her own life. Unfounded though it had been, she had lacked the courage to challenge the gossips. Eventually it had made her work impossible and she had left a job she had really liked.

She picked up the plastic cup and pressed the 'coffee, no milk or sugar' option. 'I wish this machine didn't splutter so', she remonstrated. She rather hoped she could divert the conversation, but in her heart she knew that at some point she would have to decide whether to make a stand against the destructive pattern of groundless chatter.

There is a poignant scene in the film *Schindler's List* when Schindler is speaking with the Commandant of the camp, subtly trying to persuade him that he can choose to exercise power as mercy. When Schindler has gone the Commandant stands before a mirror. He lifts his hand and puts it into the shape of the sign of a blessing. Then he turns it, making it into a gun. He practises before the mirror, playing with the ideas of blessing and shooting, life or death.

A young Jewish boy is cleaning the Commandant's bath, terrified that he cannot remove the stains at the edge. The Commandant speaks to him kindly, saying it does not matter. Elated, the child skips out across the square. But the Commandant, watching him from his window, suddenly picks up his rifle and with slow casualness and cold indifference shoots him.

Whilst our decisions may not be so obviously a choice between life or death, whatever our choices, large or small, each either contributes to the coming of the Kingdom or works against it.

Christ's proclamation that 'the kingdom of heaven is at hand' demands an active response from us, and an alertness to the challenge of this moment. It requires that we live as forgiving and forgiven; it pleads for an appreciation of God's presence in the ordinary everyday time of our lives and a willingness to be open to the surprising revelation of God at our feet. It also asks us to live with a vision of how Christ's command to love each other could be worked out in the 'now' decisions of our daily becoming.

The present moment is sacramental; it is the moment, the only moment, in which we can engage with the presence of Christ. Just as the ordinary bread and wine hold the presence of Christ, so it is this very ordinary day, this wet Monday morning or weary Friday afternoon, this seemingly insignificant human conversation, which contains the eternal.

Afterwards she wondered if it had been a visitation, a moment of revelation, a window into the world as it really is, if only we could become aware of it.

It was an ordinary Tuesday, nothing spectacular on the horizon, no reason to be particularly excited or exhilarated. She had been walking along the familiar route to work through an unremarkable passage which she used virtually every day; it ran between an area of grass adjoining a swimming pool and the backs of terraced houses, a brick wall of about four feet on her left and the backs of garages on her right.

Suddenly the whole area appeared illuminated, as if she were seeing the colour of the world, realizing its Technicolor vibrancy for the first time. Everything was incredibly vivid, the light slanting through the trees, the movement of the wind in the leaves, the variation of the textures of the bricks in the wall, the details of the garage doors. She was aware of herself in space, her feet's contact with the ground, the sense of movement as her arms and legs swung along, the clear piping of birdsong, the thud of a workman's hammer.

The sheer gift of life, of being alive at this moment, was overwhelming. Her whole being proclaimed the 'now-ness' of it all. This moment, this fragment of time, was her life. It was now and there was an urgency to seize it, relish it, live it.

This is the day, the kingdom of heaven is at hand and the glory of God is present in the now.

Concluding prayer

Lord, this is the day
This is the day when I could choose to live fully

Rinsing out darkened stains of long-gone wounds
Emptying festering cauldrons of resentment
Sluicing the locked gates of pent-up anger.
Lord, this is the day to
Pour oil on the troubled waters of my memory
Smooth ointment into the itching scars of hurt
Bask in the fragrance of forgiveness' balm
Live as forgiven and forgiving.

Lord, this is the day
This is the day when I could choose to live fully
Recognizing your Kingdom in each situation
Seeing your face in everyday encounters
Wrestling with spirit times of desolation.
Lord, this is the day to
Welcome each moment's unknown potential
Open myself to unexpected blessings
Be surprised by God's pervading presence.

Lord, this is the day
Lord, this is the day when I could choose to live fully
Choosing extravagant, risk-taking, love-giving life
Pledging my heart to the challenging spur of your Spirit
Committing my will to respond, to act, to change.
This is the day to
Breathe the freedom of your heady lifestyle
Walk with faith untrod and untried paths
Welcome your Kingdom into the time of today.
Amen.

Part 2
Reflections and exercises on Session 6, 'This is the day'

1 Redeeming the time
Read Hebrews 12.1–2.

(a) What are the 'sins to which you cling'? Are there patterns of prayer, thought or action which you need to relinquish in order to be free to live in the present more fully?

(b) What is 'the race' for which you are entered at present? Are you still running yesterday's events and not training for today? What would help you to focus more fully on the present challenge?

(c) The author of Hebrews advises us to fix our eyes on Jesus 'who endured the cross, making light of its disgrace'. Take time to reflect upon Christ's helplessness upon the cross.

What must it have been like to be mocked, humiliated, thrown on the scrap heap?

What anxieties must he have endured about his mother, his friends?

What regrets and remorse might he have endured?

Take time to recall occasions when you have felt helpless in the face of injustice, pain, disgrace or disappointment.

How can you redeem those moments? Is this the time to make a symbolic action to free you for the 'now'?

Is there a painful letter you might now burn, an act of reconciliation you might dare to attempt?

You may find it helpful to write down just a word or sentence to summarize these painful experiences. Put the paper in a suitable container and burn it in a safe place. You might like to say these words:

These events and people hurt me.
I feel the sadness, loss and despair of all that happened.
By burning this symbol of my memories
I choose to turn once more towards life
I choose to relinquish the hold this past has on my today
I ask for grace to heal the past and live the now.

If you have a garden you could bury the ashes and plant bulbs or a flower above them. You might like to say these words:

I bury these ashes, the symbol of my sorrow.
I plant these seeds in the now of today.
I commit my trust and hope for tomorrow.

2 Road safety for living in the now

Find a safe place to do this exercise and take sensible precautions. Perhaps you might choose to ask a friend to supervise you.

Stand facing the front. Then turn your head as far as is comfortable to look over your right shoulder. Walk forward, still looking over your shoulder.

How does this feel? What difficulties do you experience?

Stand facing the front. Now walk backwards whilst still facing the front.

How does this feel? What difficulties do you experience?

3 This is the day

Make a habit of using one simple phrase at the beginning of each day to remind yourself of the sacredness of the 'now'.

Return to the phrase when opportunity allows in the day. You may wish to use one of these phrases:

- 'This is the day the Lord has made. Let us rejoice and be glad in it.'
- 'The Kingdom of Heaven is at hand.'
- 'I am with you always till the end of time.'
- 'Behold, I make all things new.'

4 Choosing life

Select a time at the end of the day when you can be still and silent for five to ten minutes.

Reflect on the choices you have made during the day. Consider relationships, work, decisions, casual encounters, home responsibilities.

Which were choices for life? Take time to savour and value them and give thanks.

Which were choices for death? Take time to forgive yourself and others. Is there any action you need to take to redeem those choices?

Reflect on the signs of 'the Kingdom' you have observed today, perhaps in unselfish generosity, courage in the face of adversity, patience in frustrations. Recognize and give thanks for these times.

Reflect on what parts of today have been eternal. Give thanks for times of sharing solidarity with others, love, experiences of beauty and joy.

Guidance for group leaders

1 Self-care

Leading a group is a gift of generosity and involves the giving of time, skills and energy. Group members can sometimes disclose intimate information within the secure context of a trusting group which meets regularly. Ensure that you have the support structures to refer people on to others for help should they need it. Ensure that you have someone outside of the group who can act in a supervisory role and with whom you can share your own insights and feelings if necessary.

2 Clarifying the purpose of the time together

The way you adapt the material, the venue and the numbers in the group will vary according to whether you are using the material as the basis for a discussion group or for quiet meditation. Make this clear in the flyers/posters about the group. For example:

- The focus of the group will be 'Time and our spiritual journey'. This is an occasional group. Following the planning meeting, the group will meet six times over a period of six months for shared quiet reflection based on the book *Time: God's Gift in a Busy World*.
- The focus of the group will be 'Time and our spiritual journey'. This is a weekly discussion group which will meet for an initial meeting followed by six consecutive weekly meetings and will involve both discussion and short times for reflection.

- The focus of the group will be 'Time and our spiritual journey'. This Quiet Day will be led by . . . and will use some of the material in the book *Time: God's Gift in a Busy World*.

3 Preparation

Do allow yourself sufficient time to read the book and familiarize yourself with its format before the first Session.

If the material is being used for a discussion group, there are several decisions about the way you use the material which will need to be made at the first meeting.

Will the group . . .

- read all of Part 1 of each Session and come with their comments? The group could then do one activity together or individually at the meeting;
- read all of Part 1 of each Session *and* do one reflective activity, and come prepared to share comments on both the section and their chosen activity?

4 An opening meeting for discussion groups

Ensure that those attending know how to get to the venue and the start time. Arrange that this session is relatively short (perhaps an hour) and is to enable the group to meet each other, introduce the material, share expectations and fears and set the working boundaries of the group. This always takes longer than expected and cannot reasonably be incorporated into the first Session, especially if the group are strangers. A cup of tea or coffee can ease the introductions.

Ice breaker

You will need a piece of paper and a pen for each member of the group and an egg timer.

Ask the group to jot down the first words which come into their heads when you say the word 'time'. (Allow just one minute.)

Ask the group to share what they have put down with a partner. Set the egg timer for this; each person is allowed an egg timer's worth of speaking time (approximately three minutes each).

Invite the group to share their insights and comments together. In what ways are their comments similar? How do their insights differ? (Allow twenty minutes.)

Introducing the material

Allow time for the group to look at the Introduction to the book and to familiarize themselves with the format.

Discuss and agree the way your group will use the book and what they will do before each meeting (see above). Be sensitive to the fact that some people may have more time than others.

Introduce the idea of keeping a journal to note down ideas as suggested in the Introduction. Request that members bring their journal, paper, pen and Bible to each meeting.

Boundaries and confidentiality

Agree the starting and finishing times of the group. Be realistic about the times the group can make and then *keep to them*. It can be very wearying for the group if members continually arrive late or if the group goes on later than the agreed stop time, so agree the basic format of the meeting. For example: 'Coffee/tea is available from 7.00. We start promptly at 7.15 and finish at 9.30' or 'We start at 7.30 and finish at 9.00. Coffee is available afterwards until 9.30.' It is helpful if the host is a different person from the group leader so that responsibilities are shared.

Make it clear that whatever is shared in the group is confidential to the group and should go no further. Reassure the group that no one will be obliged to share anything they do not want to, or to disclose the comments they have written in their journal.

5 Enabling and encouraging

Some members may have a tendency to dominate whilst others may be hesitant about speaking in public, and a balance needs to be kept to make sure that all members of the group have an opportunity to contribute to the discussion. Encourage those who speak by thanking them for their contribution and perhaps highlighting something which others might like to add to. Phrases such as 'I wonder if anyone else would like to contribute?' or 'Does anyone else have a similar experience they could share?' may help.

6 Making a focus point

You may like to provide a simple central display which helps the group to focus on the theme of the week. This could be a small low table covered with a cloth or piece of material on which the group assembles various items at the beginning of the session. Some suggestions for each week are given in the section 'Closing worship' at the end of this book, but encourage the group to use their imagination as to what they might bring. The first week the group leader may have to initiate this, but encourage the group to participate by bringing their own items to put on the table during the following weeks. Try to make time for members to explain briefly what their item signifies for them.

7 During the meeting

Have a clear idea of the pattern of the meeting and an approximate time each part of the meeting might take. A possible format might be:

Review

A brief review of the material covered in the last Session.

Introduction

Use the summary ('This Session explores . . .') at the beginning of the Session to introduce this week's theme. Invite participants to put symbols of the theme on the focus table, encouraging members to say why they have chosen that item.

Sharing the stories in the Session

How did the stories in this Session affect you?

In what ways could you identify with the stories?

Are there similar stories from your own life which you feel are related and which you would like to share?

Sharing any particular insight from the Session

Which particular points of this Session have been especially relevant to your experience?

Which aspects about time had you not reflected on before?

In what ways might you reassess your attitude towards time and your behaviour in the light of your reflections and our discussions?

Doing the exercise

Depending on the exercise chosen, this might be done individually, in pairs or as a group. Give a clear indication of how much time is available.

Sharing the fruits of the time

Use this section to help everyone draw their thoughts and feelings together. The group may appreciate a few minutes to jot ideas and insights in their journal, but do give an opportunity to share insights together.

Closing prayer and possibly music

Closing the meeting

Allow time to bring the meeting to a close. Remember to:

- clarify the tasks to be accomplished before the next meeting, pointing out the Session to be read and the agreed activity, if necessary;
- highlight any particular equipment needed for next week and arrange who is responsible for bringing it;
- remind everyone of the theme for the next meeting and make suggestions for the time theme table.

8 A Quiet Day

If the material is being used for a group Quiet Day, much of the above guidance is relevant but the leader might also consider the following:

- The structure of the day and the time available. This will influence how much of the material to use. There is sufficient material for two linked Quiet Days, each of three Sessions. A suggested timetable is given below but there are many different ways to adapt the material.
- Whether the leader only has access to the book and introduces each Session, or each participant has their own copy to read at leisure.
- The experience and expectations of the group and their familiarity with Quiet Days and retreats. For some people,

being silent in the company of others can be a new experience and may feel threatening.

- The balance of silence and talking. Is there to be sharing after each Session and then periods of silence? Are mealtimes in silence? Is there a designated area for uninterrupted silence?
- The freedom to miss Sessions and take longer on reflective exercises.
- The availability of someone with whom to speak confidentially if issues arise for participants during the day.

A suggested timetable might be:

- 9.30–10.00: Arrivals and coffee available.
- 10.00–10.15: Introduction to the day, sharing of experiences and expectations.
- 10.15–11.00: Session 1 or 4.
- 11.00–11.30: Reflective exercise on Session 1 or 4.
- 11.30–11.45: Mid-morning coffee break.
- 11.45–12.30: Session 2 or 5.
- 12.30–1.15: Reflective exercise on Session 2 or 5.
- 1.15–2.15: Lunch.
- 2.15–3.00: Session 3 or 6.
- 3.00–3.30: Reflective exercise on Session 3 or 6.
- 3.30–4.00: Gathering the fruits and closing prayer.
- 4.00: Tea and depart.

Music and poems for further reflection

There is such a wealth of music and poetry, so any choice is entirely personal. The following are therefore only tentative suggestions and simply the music and poetry which I have found helpful for myself in relationship to these themes at this point in my time.

Wherever possible, details of the original publications have been given. However, many of the poems listed can be found on poetry websites or in anthologies. The following anthologies were particularly helpful in compiling this selection:

Being Alive: The Sequel to Staying Alive, ed. Neil Astley (Tarset, Bloodaxe Books, 2004).

Let the Poet Choose, ed. James Gibson (London, Harrap, 1973).

The Lion Christian Poetry Collection, compiled by Mary Batchelor (Oxford, Lion Publishing, 2001).

The Nation's Favourite Poems (London, BBC Worldwide, 1996).

Encouraging group members to make an anthology of words and music as you go along may be a worthwhile additional way of reflecting on the theme.

Session 1: There is no time

Music

Satie, *Gymnopédies* 1
Taizé Chant, 'Be still and know that I am God'
Track entitled 'Breathe on me' from CD *Bliss*
Track 'A Hundred Thousand Angels' from CD of same name.
   Both CDs available from www.blissfulmusic.com
'God it was who said to Abraham' from *Love from Below* by
   Iona Worship Group

Poems

Armitage, Simon, 'Killing time #2' in *Travelling Songs*
   (London, Faber and Faber, 2002).
Blunden, Edmund, 'God's time' in *Let the Poet Choose*, ed.
   James Gibson (London, Harrap, 1973).
Duguid, Sandra, 'Be still and know' in *The Lion Christian
   Poetry Collection*, compiled by Mary Batchelor (Oxford,
   Lion Publishing, 2001).
Miyashina, Toki, 'The Lord is my Pace Setter' in *Psalm 23:
   An anthology* compiled by K. H. Strange and R. G. E.
   Sandbach (Edinburgh, St Andrew Press, 1978).

Session 2: What time is it?

Music

Elgar, *Nursery Suite* (Aubade)
Elgar, *Enigma Variations* (Variation 1, Caroline Alice)
Dohnányi, *Variations on a Nursery Song*

Poems

Cope, Wendy, 'Names' in *Serious Concerns* (London, Faber
   and Faber, 1992).

Fowler, Lona, 'The middle time' (poem published in *Student Leadership Journal*, Fall 2003, and may be accessed through www.intervarsity.org/slj).

Holbrook, David, 'Calms of the sunshine', *Let the Poet Choose*, ed. James Gibson (London, Harrap, 1973).

Jennings, Elizabeth, 'Mary's Magnificat' in *Consequently I Rejoice* (Manchester, Carcanet, 1977).

Lewin, Ann, 'Still growing' in *By the Way* (Winchester, Optimum Litho, 1990).

MacNeice, Louis, 'Prayer before birth' in *Selected Poems of Louis MacNeice* (London, Faber and Faber, 1964).

Wordsworth, William, 'Intimations of immortality from recollections of early childhood' in *The Oxford Book of English Verse 1250–1900*, ed. A. T. Quiller-Couch (Oxford, Clarendon Press, 1907).

Session 3: Sensing time's rhythms

Music

Vivaldi, *The Four Seasons*

Delius, 'Summer Night on the River'; 'On Hearing the First Cuckoo in Spring'

Ravel, *Daybreak*

Alternatively, you may like to choose a variety of rhythms from Strauss's waltzes, military marches, or the syncopated rhythms of jazz music.

Poems

De la Mare, Walter, 'Silver' in *Collected Rhymes and Verse* (London, Faber and Faber, 1978).

Hopkins, Gerard Manley, 'Spring' in *Gerard Manley Hopkins: The Major Works* (Oxford, Oxford World's Classics, 2002).

Oliver, Mary, 'The summer day' in *New and Selected Poems* (Boston, MA, Beacon Press, 1992).

Thomas, Dylan, 'Poem in October' in *Dylan Thomas' Collected Poems* (London, Phoenix, 2003).

Session 4: When time stands still

Music

Vaughan Williams, 'The Lark Ascending'
Barber, *Adagio for Strings*, Op. 11
Tavener, 'Alleluia' (Song for Athene)
Massenet, 'Meditation de Thaïs'

Poems

Auden, W. H., 'Twelve songs, IX, Stop all the clocks' in *Collected Shorter Poems* (London, Faber and Faber, 1966).

Browning, Elizabeth Barrett, 'How do I love thee?' in *Sonnets from the Portuguese* (London and New York, Doubleday, 1991).

Donne, John, 'The good-morrow' in *The Complete Poetry and Selected Prose of John Donne*, ed. Charles M. Coffin (London, Modern Library, Random House, 2001).

Hopkins, Gerard Manley, 'Pied beauty' in *Gerard Manley Hopkins: The Major Works* (Oxford, Oxford World's Classics, 2002).

Oliver, Mary, 'Look and see' in *Why I Wake Early* (Boston, MA, Beacon Press, 2004).

Stallworthy, Jon, 'The almond tree' in *Rounding the Horn: Collected Poems* (Manchester, Carcanet, 1998).

Session 5: The time of your lives

Music

For this Session encourage participants to bring music which speaks to them most powerfully about a period of their life, whether this is pop music, tunes from musicals, or classical music.

Poems

Dunmore, Helen, 'Glad of these times' in *Being Alive: The Sequel to Staying Alive*, ed. Neil Astley (Tarset, Bloodaxe Books, 2004).

Fanthorpe, U. A., 'A wartime education' in *Collected Poems 1978–2003* (Calstock, Peterloo Poets, 2005).

Owen, Wilfred, 'Anthem for doomed youth' in *The Poems of Wilfred Owen*, ed. Edmund Blunden (London, Chatto & Windus, 1931).

Smith, Ken, 'Message on the machine' in *Shed: Poems 1980–2001* (Tarset, Bloodaxe Books, 2002).

Session 6: This is the day

Music

Copland, 'Fanfare for the Common Man'
Widor, 'Toccata'

Poems

Frost, Robert, 'The road not taken' in *The Poetry of Robert Frost*, ed. Edward Connery Lathem (London, Jonathan Cape, 1969).

Heaney, Seamus, 'Blackberry picking' in *Opened Ground: Selected Poems 1966–1996* (London, Faber and Faber, 1999).

Music and poems

Housman, A. E., 'Loveliest of trees' in *Collected Poems* (London, Jonathan Cape, 1939).

Jennings, Elizabeth, 'Summer and time' in *Selected Poems* (Manchester, Carcanet, 1979).

Larkin, Philip, 'An Arundel tomb' in *Collected Poems* (London, Faber and Faber, 2003).

Closing worship

This worship is designed to be used at the completion of all six sessions.

Before the Worship you will need to

- Decide who is the Worship Leader.
- Make sure the Worship Leader is familiar with the text and development of the worship.
- Organize the Worship Focus.
- Arrange for different people to bring different items to add to the display during worship and say the Participant's words.
- Familiarize everyone with the response, 'May we be still in your presence and live in your time.'
- Arrange for two Voices to read 'This is the day'.
- Choose music/hymns if you are going to include this.

The Worship Focus

If possible arrange the group in a circle so that everyone can see the Worship Focus. Depending on the space available, you may like to make the Focus simply a small table covered with a cloth or create a mandala using different swathes of material (lining material is relatively cheap and can be bought in a wide variety of colours).

Choose colours which help the group to identify with the different seasons of the year and perhaps suggest the liturgical seasons. For example, gold and brown shades for autumn, bright holly red and green for winter, primrose yellow and light green for spring, purple for Lent, shades of blue for summer. On each colour place just one item to help suggest the passing of the seasons and events: e.g. some dried leaves or flowers, a Christmas card, a cross, a Remembrance Day poppy, a pair of beach sandals. Leave space for other items to be added as each Session of the course is remembered during the worship. Suggestions for other items are given below.

The Worship

WL = Worship Leader. P = Participant(s).

WL   Gracious God, the Creator and Giver of all time
Alpha and Omega
We gather within the wonder of time
To seek reconciliation and peace with past times
To give thanks for the time of our lives
To seek guidance for the choices we make about our time
To dedicate ourselves anew to spending our lives in a greater awareness of your life-giving presence.

Hymn: the Taizé chant 'Be still and know that I am God' or a hymn of your choice.

WL   Ever Present God,
Whose Son Jesus lived on this earth experiencing all the constraints and limitations of time
We offer you those aspects of our time which long for the balm of your calming presence
Times when we feel overwhelmed by the tasks before us
Burdened by the responsibilities we have undertaken

111

Harassed by the complexities of the issues confronting us
Times when we feel that 'there is no time'.

Participant puts symbols of Session 1, 'There Is No Time', on display. Anything which suggests the organizational aspect of time: diaries, clocks, time sheets, egg timer, stop watch, calendars etc.

P   From the rising of the sun until its setting we acknowledge you as the God of all our time.

All   May we be still in your presence and live in your time.

WL   Life-giving God, who knew us before we were formed in the womb,
Who loves us from our first to our last breath
Who nurtures both our past and our future
Who welcomes and gives worth to all our ages

We offer you our past times with thanksgiving
We leave at your feet those times which crave your healing
Arouse our imaginations to respond to your creative will
Strengthen our hearts for your surprising futures

Participant puts symbols of particular stages of life on display for Session 2, 'What Time Is It?' – e.g. a photograph or artefact which portrays something of a particular stage of your life now, whether youth, middle age, or old age. This could be a photograph of a baby, a graduation, a wedding, a party at work, a holiday. It could be a prospectus of a course you are doing, your rail pass to work, or a small gardening tool.

P   From the rising of the sun until its setting we acknowledge you as the God of all our time.

All   May we be still in your presence and live in your time.

WL   Dancing God, Creator of Rhythm
Day and night, summer and winter, seedtime and harvest
Work and rest, stillness and movement,
We offer you our waking and our resting
Our dreaming and our actions
Our times of energy and times of exhaustion
The rhythms of our family life, our community, our nation
The beating cycle of our living times.

Participant puts symbols of the rhythms of the year onto display for Session 3, 'Sensing Time's Rhythm' – something which denotes the natural seasons, the liturgical seasons or the changing round of family, local and national events: e.g. autumn leaves or dried flowers, nuts, a Remembrance Day poppy, an Advent calendar, holly, a Christmas/birthday card, a spring flower, a recipe for pancakes, a small cross, an Easter card or egg, beach sandals, holiday brochures, a poster for a firework display or a carnival.

P   From the rising of the sun until its setting we acknowledge you as the God of all our time.

All   May we be still in your presence and live in your
            time.

WL   Mysterious God beyond all time
            Both light and dark
            Known and unknown
            Within us and beyond our imagining
            Revealing yourself in unexpected moments;
            Skimming flight of bird
            Thrusting cascade of water
            Swelling crescendo of music
            Insight of artist's eye.

            We offer you our times of transfiguration
            Moments of bliss, wilderness of desolation
            Spans of glimpsed glory, heart-wrenching grief
            Times beyond time.

*Participant puts symbols of Session 4, 'When Time Stands Still'
onto the display – something which represents a time in your
life when you were 'outside time': e.g. a birth announcement
card, a wedding service sheet, an obituary, a CD of special
music, a postcard of a favourite painting, a photo or a cut-out
from a magazine of a special view, a sunset, a flower.*

P   From the rising of the sun until its setting we
            acknowledge you as the God of all our time.

All   May we be still in your presence and live in your
            time.

WL   Sustaining God
            Who walks beside us through all the stories of our
            lives

Closing worship

Wisdom beyond our greatest understanding
Love redeeming our most grievous acts

We offer you the symbols of our history
Events which forged the bedrock of our being
Inventions altering life for good or ill
New knowledge posing unfamiliar questions
The challenges of an ever-changing world.

Participant puts symbols of Session 5, 'The Time of Your Lives', on display – something which represents the historical time within which you have lived and live: e.g. a memento, a newspaper cutting, a ration book, a CD of music, something invented during your lifetime, a mobile phone, a newspaper cutting about nuclear power, a packet of painkillers.

P   From the rising of the sun until its setting we acknowledge you as the God of all our time.

All   May we be still in your presence and live in your time.

WL   So this is the day . . .

Voice 1   Wake up! This is the day!

Voice 2   No, surely not. There must be some mistake.

Voice 1   Move, move, this is the day!

Voice 2   It's early yet, it cannot be the time.

Voice 1   This is the day!

Voice 2   I'm not ready yet. The house is in a mess and there's a lot on at work.

Voice 1   This is the day!

Voice 2   Besides, I'm feeling rather under par – a cold, a bit of backache . . .

Voice 1   This is the day!

Voice 2   You must be joking. It's Friday. A bad day to start a new venture.

Voice 1   This is the day!

Voice 2   Are you quite sure about this?

Voice 1   This is the day. There is no other!

Voice 2   This is the day? This is the day!

All   This is the day the Lord has made!
Let us rejoice and be glad in it.

Closing hymn or music.

Notes

1 Available as an audio cassette, a CD or a song book from the Wild Goose Resource Group, The Iona Community at www.iona.org.uk.
2 Tune: 'Jesus calls us', Scots Gaelic air, adapted. Words and arrangement by John L. Bell and Graham Maule, © 1989, 2002 WGRG, Iona Community, Glasgow G2 3DH, Scotland.
3 Michel Quoist, 'Lord, I have time' in *Prayers of Life* (Gill & Macmillan, 1963).
4 Dag Hammarskjöld, *Markings*, trans. W. H. Anden and Leif Sjöberg (Faber and Faber, 1964), p. 87.
5 Harold Owen, *Journey from Obscurity* (Oxford University Press, 1963), vol. 1.
6 Henry Twells, 'Time's paces' in *Uncommon Prayers for Younger People* (Hodder & Stoughton, 1953).
7 Brother Ramon, *When They Crucified My Lord* (Bible Reading Fellowship, 1999).

The Society for Promoting Christian Knowledge (SPCK) was founded in 1698. Its mission statement is:

To promote Christian knowledge by

- **Communicating the Christian faith in its rich diversity;**
- **Helping people to understand the Christian faith and to develop their personal faith; and**
- **Equipping Christians for mission and ministry.**

SPCK Worldwide serves the Church through Christian literature and communication projects in over 100 countries, and provides books for those training for ministry in many parts of the developing world. This worldwide service depends upon the generosity of others and all gifts are spent wholly on ministry programmes, without deductions.

SPCK Bookshops support the life of the Christian community by making available a full range of Christian literature and other resources, providing support for those training for ministry, and assisting bookstalls and book agents throughout the UK.

SPCK Publishing produces Christian books and resources, covering a wide range of inspirational, pastoral, practical and academic subjects. Authors are drawn from many different Christian traditions, and publications aim to meet the needs of a wide variety of readers in the UK and throughout the world.

The Society does not necessarily endorse the individual views contained in its publications, but hopes they stimulate readers to think about and further develop their Christian faith.

For further information about the Society, visit our website at *www.spck.org.uk* or write to:
SPCK, 36 Causton Street,
London SW1P 4ST, United Kingdom.